FORMATIVE ASSESSMENT
—— IN A ——
BRAIN-COMPATIBLE CLASSROOM

FORMATIVE ASSESSMENT —IN A— BRAIN-COMPATIBLE CLASSROOM

How Do We Really Know They're Learning?

MARCIA L. TATE

LearningSciencesInternational

LEARNING AND PERFORMANCE MANAGEMENT

1400 Centrepark Blvd, Suite 1000
West Palm Beach, FL 33401
717-845-6300

email: pub@learningsciences.com
learningsciences.com

21   20   19   18   17   16   1   2   3   4   5   6

Publisher's Cataloging-in-Publication Data
provided by Five Rainbows Services

Tate, Marcia L.

Formative assessment in a brain-compatible classroom / Marcia L. Tate.

pages cm

ISBN: 978-1-941112-31-1 (pbk.)

1. Educational tests and measurements. 2. Effective teaching. 3. Academic achievement.
   4. Classroom management.   I. Title.

LB3013 .T366 2015

371.26—dc23

Library of Congress Control Number: 2016934382

Table of Contents

Acknowledgments

At the end of many workshops or classes that I teach, I am assessed. Teachers fill out evaluation forms, which rate the content and delivery of what I have taught. I am grateful for the feedback since it enables me to improve my practice. Feedback to students is also extremely important if students are to improve performance, but that feedback should not be doled out in an atmosphere of threat and anxiety. We are at a time in education when students are being constantly assessed, and major evaluative decisions are being made based on those assessments. I owe a debt of gratitude to those teachers who already give students multiple and varied opportunities to show that they are learning. My hope is that every teacher will follow suit after reading this book.

I am deeply grateful for family members and other educators who have supported me through the years and assisted me with writing over thirteen books, all of which are best sellers.

To Tyrone, my husband of over thirty-five years, my biggest critic and best friend. Your timely advice and unwavering support has only made me a stronger person and a better presenter.

To my dearest children—Jennifer, Jessica, and Christopher. Your stories are an integral part of this book since you exemplify the variety of learning styles that exist in any classroom; all three of you needed both traditional and authentic ways to show what you learned. I dedicate this book to you and to my six beautiful grandchildren, who I pray will have teachers who use a variety of ways for them to show what they are learning, as well.

To the associates who present for our company, Developing Minds, Inc. Many thanks for equipping teachers with brain-compatible strategies, which make teaching and learning so memorable that assessment in their classrooms is never a threat.

To our administrative assistants, Carol Purviance and Fran Rodrigues, thank you for your strong interpersonal skills, your exemplary work ethic, and the feedback you provide daily, which enable me to reflect on my performance and become better at what I do!

Learning Sciences International would like to thank the following reviewers:

Gay F. Barnes
2012 Alabama Teacher of the Year
Horizon Elementary School
Madison, Alabama

Cathy Cartier
2013 Missouri Teacher of the Year
Affton School District
St. Louis, Missouri

Karyn Collie Dickerson
2014 North Carolina Teacher of the Year
Grimsley High School
Greensboro, North Carolina

Mary Eldredge-Sandbo
2010 North Dakota Teacher of the Year
United Public School District #7
Des Lacs, North Dakota

George E. Goodfellow
2008 Rhode Island Teacher of the Year
Scituate High School
North Scituate, Rhode Island

Jen Haberling
2009 Michigan Teacher of the Year
Baldwin Street Middle School
Hudsonville, Michigan

Daniele Massey
2013 Teacher of the Year
Department of Defense Education
   Activity
Quantico, Virginia

Kristen Merrell
2012 Missouri Teacher of the Year
Lee's Summit R-7 School District
Lee's Summit, Missouri

Yung Romano
2010 Alabama Teacher of the Year
Strawberry Crest High School
Dover, Florida

Kathleen Schaeffer
2010 Nevada Teacher of the Year
Bob Miller Middle School
Henderson, Nevada

Michelle S. Switala
2010 Pennsylvania Teacher of
   the Year
Pine-Richland High School
Gibsonia, Pennsylvania

About the Author

Marcia L. Tate is the former executive director of professional development for DeKalb County Schools in Decatur, Georgia. During her thirty-year career with the district, she was a classroom teacher, reading specialist, language arts coordinator, and staff development executive director. Marcia was named Staff Developer of the Year for the state of Georgia, and her department was selected to receive the Exemplary Program Award for the state.

Marcia is currently an educational consultant and has presented her workshops to over 450,000 administrators, teachers, parents, and community leaders from all over the United States and the world, including Australia, Canada, Egypt, Hungary, Oman, New Zealand, Singapore, and Thailand. Participants in her workshops claim that they are some of the best ones they have ever attended.

She is the author of the following eight best sellers: *Worksheets Don't Grow Dendrites: 20 Instructional Strategies That Engage the Brain* (3rd ed.); *"Sit & Get" Won't Grow Dendrites: 20 Professional Learning Strategies That Engage the Adult Brain* (2nd ed.); *Reading and Language Arts Worksheets Don't Grow Dendrites: 20 Literacy Strategies That Engage the Brain* (2nd ed.); *Mathematics Worksheets Don't Grow Dendrites: 20 Numeracy Strategies That Engage the Brain, PreK–8*; *Science Worksheets Don't Grow Dendrites: 20 Instructional Strategies That Engage the Brain*; *Shouting Won't Grow Dendrites: 20 Techniques to Detour Around the Danger Zones* (2nd ed.); *Preparing Children for Success in School and Life: 20 Ways to Increase Your Child's Brain Power*; and *Social Studies Worksheets Don't Grow Dendrites: 20 Instructional Strategies That Engage the Brain*. Marcia models the twenty strategies in her books to actively engage her audiences. She has also written a number of published articles and chapters that have been included in other books.

Marcia received her bachelor's degree in psychology and elementary education from Spelman College in Atlanta, her master's in remedial reading from the University of Michigan in Ann Arbor, and her specialist and doctorate degrees in educational leadership from Georgia State University and Clark Atlanta University, respectively. Spelman College awarded her the Apple Award for Excellence in the field of education.

Marcia is married to Tyrone Tate and is the proud mother of three children, Jennifer, Jessica, and Christopher. If she had known how wonderful it would be to be a grandmother, Marcia would have had her six grandchildren, Aaron, Aidan, Christian, Maxwell, Roman, and Shiloh, before she had her children. She and her husband own the company Developing Minds, Inc. and can be contacted by calling the company at (770) 918-5039, by emailing her at marciata@bellsouth.net, or by visiting the website at www.developing mindsinc.com.

Introduction

While I was in the process of writing this book, I was simultaneously listening to a television newscast regarding a group of ten educators from a major school district who were being accused of racketeering for falsifying the state standardized test results of students. It appeared that the cheating practice in this district dated as far back as 2005 and initially involved 180 teachers in forty-four schools. County-level administrators were also accused of not renewing the certification of educators who refused to participate in changing students' scores. The superintendent of the district was also charged, but she became ill and passed away before she could stand trial. Some administrators and teachers entered into plea deals, while others were advised by their attorneys to fight the charge in court. The court cases lasted for many months, with testimony from over one hundred witnesses.

According to the newscast, the verdict had just come in for the educators. Nine of the ten were found guilty, and the judge encouraged them to consider a plea deal prior to sentencing. He advised them to accept the plea deal since the specifications of the deal would not be as harsh as the actual sentence he would impose. However, one condition of the plea deal would be that each educator would have to admit his or her guilt. Several of the nine took the deal, while others refused to admit their guilt and were sentenced by the judge. The harshest sentences involved twenty years, with an incarceration period of seven years and the balance on probation, two thousand hours of community service, and a $25,000 fine. The most lenient sentence involved five years of probation, including one year of 7 p.m. to 7 a.m. home confinement, one thousand hours of community service, and a $5,000 fine. Several days later, it was announced that the judge was reconsidering his three harshest sentences (Lowry, 2015).

Why am I relating this story in a book on assessment? First, as an educator for over forty years, I became emotionally connected to the case itself. I would never condone what these administrators and teachers did! The judge even commented that he thought that hundreds or thousands of children had been harmed by their actions. However, I do wonder why these educators felt the need to do what they did. I am sure that this is not an isolated instance of falsifying test results occurring across our country. When teachers' reputations and jobs are in jeopardy, people who would never think of breaking the law may consider doing so. I had to ask myself this question: When we measure teacher performance by student assessment data, are we putting so much pressure on educators today that teachers see no alternative other than to cheat to get the results they seek? In the next section of this introduction, we will discuss the fact that students often see test results as tangible, visible evidence of their worth and value. Could it be that some teachers experience that same visualization?

The good news is that none of the events in the above scenario needed to have happened! It is the purpose of this book to enable teachers to put practices in place that will increase the likelihood that students will do well on teacher-made, end-of-course, and standardized tests and, more important, demonstrate that they are really learning what the teacher is teaching. Should we be teaching just for high traditional test results or also to facilitate students' abilities to remember the content long after the tests are over? After all, is the latter not the true purpose of schooling?

Assessment Versus Student Worth

In the beginning of the assessment workshop I teach, which, by the way, has the same name as this book, I read aloud a wonderful story called *First Grade Takes a Test*, by Miriam Cohen (2006). Thanks to the document camera, I am even able to show my class the pictures. This is a children's book with a much deeper meaning for teachers and administrators. It is the delightful story of a class of first graders who are required to take a standardized test. Most of the students find the test difficult and, in desperation, begin to do things like draw in answers since the correct one, in their estimation, is not among the answer choices. In another instance, a student named Sammy, when faced with the question *What do firemen do?* responds to another student that firemen get your head out when it is stuck, since that is what happened to his uncle who had his head stuck in a pipe. However, none of the multiple-choice answers say that, so he does not know which answer to mark.

One student by the name of Anna Marie, however, keeps telling everyone that the test was easy! Weeks after the test is long forgotten by the first graders, a woman from the principal's office comes back to the class and selects one student to be placed in the gifted class. Guess who it is? Anna Marie, of course! Once she is selected and the students understand why she is chosen, they become angry and begin to refer to themselves as *dummies*. The teacher reassures them that the test doesn't begin to tell all of the things that the students are capable of doing, like building things, drawing pictures, and helping one another—in other words, showing what they know in more authentic ways. In time, the students come to realize that each is smart in his or her own way, and the students' confidence and faith in their abilities are restored.

First Grade Takes a Test is fictitious. However, when you have lived the story, it takes on a much deeper meaning. You see, my Anna Marie is my daughter Jessica, who qualified for the gifted program in school and thought that most standardized tests she took were extremely easy. Growing up along with her was her younger brother, Christopher, who, due to his inability to score high on most standardized measures, began to think that he was indeed a dummy. Despite the fact that his father and I reminded him that he was gifted in other ways, such as his ability to draw, assemble things, or make use of technology, it didn't make one bit of difference. At his school and schools around the United States, the measure of a student's true ability is determined by the traditional tests they are required to take. Chris did not fare well on these measures of assessment. He has characteristics of attention deficit and does not truly show what he knows when his only option is a multiple-choice test. As time went on, Chris began to take on the characteristics of what he perceived were those of a dummy, and he started to hang around at school with other students whom he thought possessed those same characteristics. His grades and confidence plummeted, while he watched his sister graduate from a gifted magnet high school and enroll in an Ivy League college, where she continued to excel.

When I tell this story in class and show the pictures of my children, I cannot begin to tell you how many participants in my workshops approach me at the first break and admit that they, too, have a Christopher. The name may be different, but the characteristics are the same. Isn't it odd that of the people who talk to me about their struggling child, at least 80 percent of those children are male? We will follow the true saga of Jessica and Christopher throughout this book since they represent all the students who have two very different ways of acquiring information.

Could it be that with only one type of assessment, we may never know if some students are learning? If students, like my son, view assessment results as visible evidence of their value and worth, what are we doing to their confidence and their lives when they consistently fail? Could this have anything to do with the fact that there are more males than females in special education classes, more males than females in remedial reading classes, more males than females currently leaving school prior to graduation, and fewer males than females enrolling in and graduating from college? While the number of American students diagnosed with ADD has increased more than seven times since 1990, almost 80 percent of those taking medication for the disorder are male (*Pay Closer Attention*, 2004). According to A.N. James (2015), author of *Teaching the Male Brain*, it may be perfectly normal for boys, particularly pubescent boys, to show more impulsive behaviors and an inability to maintain attention. In the fifth edition of *The Diagnostic and Statistical Manual*, published by the American Psychiatric Association, characteristics that can be attributed to perfectly normal boys—such as increased activity level, impulsiveness due to immaturity, the need to handle materials, and their preference for looking at things and not people—could be identified in classrooms as attentional problems (James, 2015).

Do We Really Know They're Learning?

When I worked as an instructional coordinator for a major school district in Georgia, I served as a member of a committee designated to determine a future school calendar. In our discussion, a proposal was made to end the first semester prior to the Christmas holiday break. While I did not disagree with the proposition, I thought the rationale for the suggestion was interesting. High school teachers on the committee agreed that if the first semester did not end prior to the holidays, students would not be able to recall content over the two-week break. As a proponent of brain research, it occurred to me that if students could not retain their content over the two weeks of the holiday break, how would they ever remember the content long enough to use it during the following semester or during subsequent years? I began to consider the proposition that teaching may be geared for high test performance, while sacrificing students' long-term retention.

I am an example of this phenomenon. I made As in all of my social studies classes in elementary school. I also made As in any subject related to social studies in high school. There were no middle schools in my school district at that time. When I wrote a book several years ago for social studies teachers, I secured the assistance of several experts in the field since my knowledge of historical events is very limited. You may be asking, *How could you have made As and yet not recall much of the information later in your educational career?* The answer is simple: I crammed for exams. If you really are truthful, you know there were times when you did as well. We memorized facts, names, dates, and ideas, but only long enough to pass the subsequent tests.

Let me describe the majority of my social studies classrooms. Visualize this! My teachers called on students randomly to read parts of chapters aloud while the remainder of the class followed along in the text. Listening to classmates read at varying levels of proficiency was deadly! Then we were asked to answer the questions at the end of the chapter in writing and turn our papers in at the end of the class period for a grade. I would return home with my textbooks and any notes I had taken during the occasional lectures and memorize what I thought was going to be on the test. In most instances, I was correct and made excellent grades on the exams. To recall how much I truly still remember is another story!

How do we really know that students are learning? For Christopher, a traditional paper/pencil test alone will not provide you with that information. For gifted Jessica, the same test may not provide you with that information either. Let me give you an example. When Jess was in high school, I noticed that she was spending time during her homework memorizing the answers to 300 multiple-choice questions. When I asked her what she was doing, she told me that 100 of the 300 questions would appear on a chemistry final exam, but since she had no idea which 100, she was memorizing the answers to all of them. When I selected one question and asked her to explain why (d) was the correct answer, she could not do it. Even if she scored very high on her final exam (which, by the way, she did), would we really know if Jessica had learned chemistry?

Contents of This Book

By the time you finish reading this book, you will have numerous ways to tell whether your students are truly learning what you need them to know, understand, or be able to do. Each chapter asks and answers a question, the same way that teachers should begin each planned lesson. We will examine the *what*, *why*, and *how* of assessment. We will begin the *what* by differentiating between some terms that can be easily confused by the reader—terms such as *assessment* versus *evaluation*, *formative* versus *summative assessment*, and *traditional* versus *authentic assessment*. Then we will examine the *why*, which presents several reports and research studies that support why teachers should use a variety of assessment types if they are to truly surmise whether students are learning. The remainder of the book explores the answers to the following *how* questions.

- How can I create a brain-compatible classroom that fosters success and helps instill in students the confidence to do well when they are assessed?

- How can I plan my lessons so that students know what they should know and be able to do?

- How can I ask effective questions that really tell me if my students are learning what I need them to learn?

- How can I create the most effective teacher-made, traditional tests?

- How can I tell before, during, and after the lesson what my students know?

Many teachers avoid product and performance types of assessments that cannot be easily graded. Yet, if these are not also included, we will never know if some students are learning. Therefore, two chapters will be devoted to the importance of developing checklists and rubrics to assess students' learning. Students also need time to peer- and self-assess, and one chapter is devoted to that topic. In summary, I offer four ways for students to succeed at any assessment.

Since the brain theory of primacy/recency states that the brain tends to remember what it encounters first and last, before the middle, the end of each chapter contains a chapter summary that addresses the answer to the initial chapter question. Teachers in professional learning communities (PLCs) can discuss the answers to the reflective questions as they examine student assessment data and plan for increased student achievement.

With over forty years in the field of education, I have been entrenched in assessment since the beginning of my career. As time has progressed, however, the time I have spent preparing students to be tested and the testing itself has increased exponentially. In his book *Revolutionize Assessment*, Rick Stiggins (2014) provides a wonderful summary to this part of the introduction when he relates what we already know about state assessments: (1) the time students spend taking state assessments has increased substantially; (2) the tests themselves have increased in length, with students becoming exhausted often before they get to the questions that make a difference to their score; (3) the exams are filled with ambiguous questions that even educators cannot agree on; and (4) tests have put students' brains in states of such high stress that tears are shed.

I once read an article that contained this quote: *You can't fatten a pig by continuing to weigh him.* It made me wonder whether we are spending so much time weighing (testing) our students and not enough time fattening (teaching) them. I contend that, if done correctly, students can be both fattened and weighed.

What Are the Types of Assessment?

Before we begin to explore in depth the concept of formative assessment in a brain-compatible classroom, let us review some terminology that shows up consistently in the literature. This will ensure that we are all on the same page, as it relates to our understanding of how we know that students are really learning.

Assessment Versus Evaluation

Some educators use the terms *assessment* and *evaluation* interchangeably. However, they are not the same. Assessment consists of all the tools (i.e., tests, observations, class work, and presentations) that teachers use to gather information about the effectiveness of teaching and learning. Assessment is ongoing and can consist of (1) determining what students already know before beginning a unit of study or the development of a skill, (2) analyzing the results of a student's current performance, and (3) formulating a plan to help students learn the things that they do not currently know (Burke, 2010). During assessment, teachers use diagnostic data to determine students' academic and social needs and then plan appropriate curricular opportunities and instructional strategies to meet those predetermined needs.

Evaluation, on the other hand, occurs when one collects and examines assessment data and information and makes decisions about what it shows. Based on assessment data, evaluative decisions regarding student promotion or reten-tion, levels of teacher or school effectiveness, or proficiency on state or national standards are determined. Unsound assessment practices can, therefore, result in unsound evaluative decisions. For example, when a student's performance on a single standardized test is used solely to determine whether that student can be promoted to the next grade, this evaluative decision could be based on an unsound assessment practice.

Here is an example. It is ironic that on the same day I am writing this chap-ter of the book, my other daughter, Jennifer, who is now an academic coach for an elementary school, is relating a recent story. It is the day that students in her building are scheduled to take the state standardized test. However, when she gets to school, she notices that no one is in the building. Since she always arrives very early, she does not think much of it, but she realizes that it is very unusual for no one to be around. She is then told by the bomb squad to evacuate the building immediately because of an anonymous bomb scare. She runs to join the small group of teachers and students who are standing across the street. No sooner had the school been checked out and all teachers and students returned to their respective classrooms when the person called again and the process had to be repeated. Now, keep in mind that this was originally scheduled as a day of testing. The administrative team had the presence of mind to reschedule the testing, but just imagine how students' brains would have been affected if they had been required to take the test regardless of what was happening in the school. No one looking at the students' subsequent test scores would know or care why the scores of some students were so low. By the way, it was later discovered that a fifth-grade student in the school was the person who called in the anonymous bomb threats. The moral of this story is that the conditions under which some students have to take tests can often influence the scores. We will discuss this phenomenon in chapter 3, when we talk about creating a brain-compatible environment conducive to learning.

Assessment does not consist of a test administered on one particular day. Assessment is a continuous, ongoing, and differentiated process to meet the needs of students. Students are allowed to improve their performance, as teach-ers improve their teaching (Burke, 2010). Evaluation usually occurs at the end of an assessment cycle. It is a student's last attempt to meet standards or course objectives. From the evidence, teachers make final decisions about stu-dent work. Those decisions are used to evaluate teacher effectiveness and prove the quality of the learning to parents, administrators, and other stakeholders (Burke, 2010).

Since the purpose of this book is to answer questions that teachers have about assessment, after each section in this chapter I will assess your ability to discern the difference between each of the terms delineated. Please take each test before you peek at the answers.

Test 1

Label the following scenarios as examples of assessment or evaluation:

1. The graduation rate for Wilson High School is two percentage points higher this year than last year.

2. The decision has been made not to promote John to the fourth grade.

3. Carlos made 90 percent on a midsemester trigonometry test.

4. The fourth-grade standardized test scores at McKinley Elementary School are lower than the state average.

5. Eighty-five percent of the class responds appropriately during questioning.

Answer Key

1. Evaluation   4. Evaluation

2. Evaluation   5. Assessment

3. Assessment

Formative Versus Summative

Since this book focuses on assessment rather than evaluation, I will distinguish between the two major forms of assessment—formative and summative. The terms are defined in accordance with the purpose each serves, the timing in which they take place, the requirements of the course itself, and the standards on which students have to demonstrate mastery.

While formative appears to be assessment for learning, summative appears to be assessment of learning, since the purpose of summative assessment is to determine final grades or proficiency levels related to state standards or course outcomes (Burke, 2010). Dylan Wiliam (2011) relates that, during formative assessment, a teacher secures information that provides the best evidence possible about what students have already learned; he then uses the information to determine what should be done next. Brookhart and Nitko (2007) make the concept of formative assessment clearer when they use a simile to define it as a loop. Students and teachers together decide on a learning target, evaluate how close or far current student work is in relation to the target, take action to move the student work closer to the target, and then do it all over again.

For assessment to be truly formative, three things must be in place (DuFour, Eaker, & Karhanek, 2010):

1. Students who are experiencing difficulty are identified.
2. Students are given additional time and support to acquire the concept or skill.
3. Students are given additional opportunities to show what they have learned.

Do these types of assessments appear to make a difference in student achievement? According to the research of John Hattie (2009), if done appropriately, formative assessment ranks fourth among all of the influences that positively impact student learning and can result in more than two years of student growth in a single academic year. Wiliam's research (2007) concluded that the minute-to-minute and day-by-day use of classroom formative assessment could increase student achievement by 0.4 to 0.7 standard deviations. These results would place the United States in the top five countries in the international rankings for achievement in math. The results of effective use of feedback from those assessments are almost equally as effective. The importance of appropriate feedback will be discussed in chapter 13.

Summative assessment typically takes place at the end of a chapter, quarter, semester, grading period, or a school year and is used for a variety of purposes, such as retention of students and evaluation of schools and districts. The purpose of summative assessment is similar to that of evaluation. This book will not deal in depth with summative assessment since formative assessment, if done correctly, leaves little doubt as to a student's final performance.

An identical assessment could even be called formative during the daily teaching and learning process and summative at the end of the grading period. In other words, the focus on the use of these measures depends on how teachers choose to use them, either during or after a lesson. Let's examine the difference in terms of their purposes. According to Burke (2010), the purpose of formative assessment is to provide both teacher and student with continuous feedback to *improve* learning during a learning segment, while the purpose of summative assessment is to evaluate a student's final effort to *prove* that learning has taken place at the conclusion of a learning segment.

This concept is made clearer through the following analogy. When I became seventeen, my father was teaching me to drive. Each time he took me out for practice, he formatively assessed me on several aspects of driving. These included my ability to start the car, stay in my lane, signal when appropriate, make left and right turns, and stop the car when I had arrived at my destination. All of these observations informed my father of my progress during the teaching process as well as what aspects of the driving process we needed to practice in the subsequent sessions.

After a number of sessions, when Dad thought I was ready, he drove me to the driver's license bureau to take my official driver's test. I considered this test my summative assessment since I either would receive or be denied my driver's license based on my performance. That performance consisted of the results of both a multiple-choice test regarding the rules of the road, which, at the time I was tested, was of the paper and pencil variety, and a performance-based driver's test, where I demonstrated my proficiency on all of the things my father had taught me. Dad was pretty sure that by the time I took my summative driving assessment, I would pass. And I did! Now, take the following assessment to test your understanding of the difference between formative and summative assessment.

Test 2

Label the following scenarios as examples of formative or summative assessment:

1. Students grade one another's homework assignment.
2. Students complete their final entries in their learning logs.
3. Cooperative groups rehearse their role-play of a scene in American history while the teacher observes.
4. Lois takes an English end-of-course test.
5. The teacher calls on volunteers and nonvolunteers to answer questions during the whole-class discussion of dominant and recessive genes.

Answer Key

1. Formative   4. Summative
2. Summative   5. Formative
3. Formative

Traditional Versus Authentic

Which came first in the world: school or brains? Of course, human beings had brains long before there was a place called school. This would seem to indicate that the initial purpose of the brain was not to enable students to make straight As or score high on a teacher-made or standardized test. The purpose of the brain was to enable the person to survive in the world. Its job was to keep the body of its owner alive!

According to Algozzine et al. (2009), when learning is applicable to students' lives, students not only become more engaged but they also feel more responsible for finishing assignments and understand the relationship between their success in school and success in the real world. Would it then not make sense that those school activities that are closer to what happens in the real world would be those that are more easily understood by the brain?

A complete picture of student growth is supported by a balance in the assessment process that includes both traditional measures (such as tests, grades, and report cards) and portfolio and performance assessments, which are more authentic (Fogarty, 2009). Authentic tasks are often more complex and require that students perform in a realistic, real-world context (Gregory & Chapman, 2013). They require that students show mastery in ways that are similar to real life. Authentic tasks include project-based learning, presentations, and role-plays.

Most students will show preferences toward one type or the other. For example, of my three children, Jessica did better when assessed through more traditional approaches. She did very well on teacher-made paper/pencil tests as well as those standardized and criterion-referenced tests that she took throughout her school career, including scoring well on the Preliminary Scholastic Aptitude Test (PSAT) and the Scholastic Aptitude Test (SAT). On the other hand, my other two, Jennifer and Christopher, showed best what they knew through more authentic measures, which included both products they created and the performances in which they engaged during their schooling. If both types had not been used to assess my children, their teachers would have never really known that they were learning. Particularly in the case of my son, there were many instances in middle and high school where Chris was unable to show what he truly knew, since the only assessment types used were the more traditional ones. On the following test, determine which assessment items are more traditional and which are more authentic.

Test 3

Label the following scenarios as examples of traditional or authentic assessment:

1. Students draw five pictures to illustrate the ways in which fractions are used in the real world.

2. Margaret and her cooperative group create a PowerPoint presentation to show their understanding of a social studies chapter, which is graded by another group.

3. Students take a fill-in-the-blank test to demonstrate their knowledge of Shakespeare's *Romeo and Juliet*.

4. William writes a composition on the theme of the novel *To Kill a Mockingbird*.

5. Students create a song, rhyme, or rap to recall the initial thirteen colonies.

Answer Key

1. Authentic   4. Authentic
2. Authentic   5. Authentic
3. Traditional

Selected Responses Versus Constructed Responses

Assessment item types can be categorized according to whether a student is required to select or construct a response. Selected responses are those where the student chooses the correct answer among several answer choices. Examples of selected-response items are multiple-choice, true/false, or matching. In the current school culture, there may be a time when students must respond appropriately to these items during the formative phase since many summative assessments adhere to this format as well. However, if these are the only assessment items given, you will never know if some students are learning what you are teaching.

There is a school of thought that students should not simply identify the correct answer or reproduce what they've seen or heard from a teacher; they should actually produce their own original work. Therefore, fortunately, there is another major category of assessment types—constructed responses. Constructed responses can be placed into two categories: products and performances. Products are nouns and consist of what students can *create* to show what they are learning. Examples of products are posters, songs, graphic organizers, PowerPoint presentations, and other creations similar to the authentic assessments listed previously.

Performances are verbs and include things that students can *do* to show that they are learning. Performance tasks are active, hands-on learning tasks that enable students to make connections to real-world situations. Examples of performances are to read aloud, solve a problem, debate an issue, role-play a scene from history, and so forth. When students are completing performance tasks, they are exercising what many are now referring to as 21st century thinking skills: this includes the ability to solve problems, think critically, analyze information, communicate orally and in writing, and exercise curiosity (Wagner, 2008).

According to Larry Ainsworth (2015), learning tasks are effective when they:

- Establish a purpose that can be applied to the real world

- Create a product or performance in response to those purposes

- Promote critical thinking through learning that is highly interactive

- Encourage a variety of approaches and solutions

- Use scoring criteria created by both teachers and students

- Include peer feedback and self-assessment

- Provide opportunities to revise work based on said feedback

- Showcase work products and performances as evidence that learning has occurred

- Apply to every grade level and content area, including those that are performance based, such as the visual and performing arts, career tech, physical education, and so forth

Oftentimes, the same activity can end up in the product and performance categories. For example, when a student writes an original song, rhyme, or rap to show what he or she is learning in class, the song, rhyme, or rap is a product. When he or she stands up in class and sings, says, or raps it, it now becomes a performance. Take the following test to assess whether you can differentiate selected from constructed responses.

Test 4

Label the following scenarios as examples of selected or constructed forms of assessment:

1. Maria takes a true/false biology test.

2. The homework assignment is to create a pizza that displays all of the parts of a human cell and bring it to school for a *Cellebration*.

3. Each cooperative group completes a Venn diagram comparing and contrasting Athenian and Spartan civilization in world history.

4. Students must match each element to its symbol on the periodic table during a paper/pencil test.

5. Students take a multiple-choice end-of-course test in English.

Answer Key

1.	Selected	4.	Selected
2.	Constructed	5.	Selected
3.	Constructed		

Student Portfolios

A portfolio is a specific collection of a student's work over a specified period. To understand this definition, visualize an artist who walks into the office of a prospective employer with a leather case full of the artist's best work. The difference is that while the artist's portfolio may contain only the finest examples, a student's portfolio should consist of samples of written work, audio and video material, and any other indication of that student's progress over time. Teachers often use portfolios to assess student growth. That growth is best reflected when a variety of assessment types is incorporated into daily instruction.

Answer to Question 1

What are the types of assessment?

Educators easily confuse some common terms related to assessment. Assessment is ongoing and involves all the tools that teachers use to gather data about the effectiveness of teaching and learning. Evaluation happens when educators gather and analyze that data and make decisions regarding what it shows.

continued ➡

Formative assessment is assessment *for* learning, since teachers are continuously collecting data and comparing it to a targeted goal, determining how far it is from the goal, and then repeating the process. Summative assessment is assessment *of* learning and occurs at the end of a grading period. Traditional types of assessment involve selected-response tests such as multiple-choice, true/false, and matching. Authentic types of assessment require students to construct their responses and can include both products and performances. A student's portfolio should include both types if we really want to know whether students are learning.

The graphic organizer in figure 1.1 provides a pictorial representation of the relationships between the concepts described in this chapter. It depicts that while both authentic and traditional types of assessment can be both formative and summative, the ultimate goal of all assessment is to evaluate students' academic achievement and teacher effectiveness.

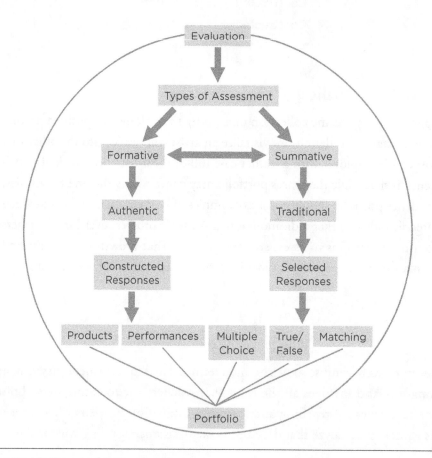

Figure 1.1: Types of assessment.

Visit www.learningsciences.com/bookresources for a reproducible version of this figure.

What Evidence Supports the Use of a Variety of Assessment Types?

There are brain theories and national studies that support the use of a variety of assessment types to tell us whether students are learning. We will consider three of them.

1. Left versus right hemisphericity
2. The theory of multiple intelligences
3. The SCANS report

Left Versus Right Hemisphericity

Early research on the brain began with the work of Dr. Roger Sperry, who attempted to assist epileptic patients in limiting their seizures to just one hemisphere of the brain. He severed the corpus callosum, the structure that joins the left and right hemispheres, in those patients. He found that while they could function rather normally, patients tended to use either the left or the right hemisphere, depending on the tasks they were attempting to perform. This discovery led Sperry to conclude that the hemispheres just might have different functions.

At one time, it was believed that the left hemisphere controlled one's ability to organize, bring structure to a task, think logically, and complete tasks that required one to demonstrate verbal or mathematical ability. Sounds a lot like *school* to me! We require students to be organized and structured. The PSAT and SAT have always consisted of verbal and mathematical sections, so many students who appear to possess strengths in the left hemisphere do better on tests of this nature.

The right hemisphere appeared to control one's ability to be creative, musical, artistic, intuitive, and global. Sounds like *real life* to me! My son, Chris, draws beautifully. I did not teach Chris to draw and neither did he learn it at school. He was born in real life knowing how to draw. Students who possessed strengths in the right hemisphere were more likely to excel in elective classes, such as art, chorus, or band. These students did not always excel on paper-and-pencil assessments, which were an integral part of academia.

The current brain research informs our practice and relates that Sperry's theory may just be too simplistic; it is also outdated. What we know now is that human beings appear to use both hemispheres of their brains all the time. For example, there appears to be a math/music connection in many brains. It seems that while music was originally thought to be associated with the right hemisphere, classical pianists and composers use many left-hemisphere characteristics as well. Many students who learn to play a musical instrument seem to do better in mathematics. Some countries in the world have very high test scores in mathematics. Those same countries also tend to have strong music and art programs. I have had Japanese parents tell me that they will arrange Suzuki violin lessons for their children in the hope that this will improve their academic achievement. According to David Sousa (2006), of all the content areas, mathematics appears to be the one most closely aligned with music. Music uses fractions for tempos, proportions, ratios, and patterns for notes and chords, counting for beats and rests, and geometry for the placement of fingers on a guitar. Yet, in the United States, the first areas to be eliminated from the curriculum due to budget cuts and increased time-on-tasks appear to be music and art since those subject areas are thought to be *fluff* and very expendable.

I received a local newspaper that told about a major school district where one-fifth of the 2012 graduating class did not graduate. The article related that of the twenty-seven high schools in the district, only two graduated all of the students in the senior class. Those two were an early college academy and a school of the performing arts. It became obvious why the students of the early college academy graduated. These students were already taking college courses. But the graduation of all the students in the senior class from the school of the performing arts only validated what I teach about the hemispheres of the brain. This staff teaches to both hemispheres. Teachers are using the strategies of music, art, and drama (formerly associated with the right hemisphere) to teach the curricular subjects of math, English, science, and social studies (formerly associated with the left hemisphere). My daughter Jessica, who had over ten years of piano lessons and sight-reads music, scored very well on the math portions of the PSAT and SAT. She spoke fluent German and was a German major in college. Her ability to sight-read music, speak fluent German, and solve higher-level math problems appears to be influenced by the spatial part of the brain, which, following the current research, spans both the left and right hemispheres.

Have you ever wondered what would happen in terms of assessment if teachers used instructional strategies that address both hemispheres of the brain to both teach and assess student learning? In this way, regardless of how students learn best, there will be a way for them to understand and retain the content. Could it be that more students, after thirteen or more years of schooling, might be qualified to walk across the stage at graduation and receive their diplomas for a job well done?

The Theory of Multiple Intelligences

Theory number two is Howard Gardner's theory of multiple intelligences. It's time for you to take another test.

Who Is This Person?

Identify these ten famous people who were not initially successful in school and/or life but who ended up making major contributions to society. Write down your answers before you check the answer key.

1. A composer handled his violin awkwardly. He preferred playing his own compositions, which his music teacher referred to as *dreadful*.

2. A cartoonist was told that he had *no creative talents* and was fired by a newspaper for not having enough new ideas.

3. An inventor was told by a teacher that he was too stupid to learn anything.

continued ➡

4. One of the smartest men in history was described by a teacher as *mentally slow, unsociable, and adrift forever in his foolish dreams*. He did not speak until age four or read until age seven.

5. One of the richest men in America was considered by his teachers as *nonstellar and unsociable*.

6. An inventor failed a class in auto mechanics, so he decided to invent the elevator.

7. A chemist ranked fifteenth in a chemistry class of twenty-two.

8. An artist turned in his textbooks upon flunking out of school, and the margins were covered in doodles.

9. This author of *War and Peace* flunked out of college and was described by his teachers as *both unable and unwilling to learn*.

10. Due to his high strikeout record, this athlete was encouraged to quit baseball.

Answer Key

1. Ludwig van Beethoven (musical intelligence)

2. Walt Disney (spatial intelligence)

3. Thomas Edison (spatial intelligence)

4. Albert Einstein (logical-mathematical intelligence)

5. Bill Gates (spatial intelligence, intrapersonal)

6. Elisha Otis (spatial intelligence)

7. Louis Pasteur (spatial intelligence)

8. Pablo Picasso (spatial intelligence)

9. Leo Tolstoy (linguistic intelligence)

10. Babe Ruth (bodily-kinesthetic intelligence)

How did you do on this test? The average score that participants in my workshops earn is 70 percent, and that score comes from working with their families or participants at their tables. Even if you did not do well, did you view your grade on this test as tangible, visible evidence of your worth and value? Probably not! Why not?

First, this test did not contain material that you had been taught. Therefore, you did not feel responsible for knowing it. Second, most educators have a positive view of their professional worth and value. After all, teachers and administrators have finished college, many have postgraduate degrees, and most are very successful in their professions.

Students do not have that same luxury. First, the majority of assessments students take in class concern content that they have already been taught and, therefore, are expected to understand and recall. If they cannot demonstrate this understanding, a low grade is recorded in the gradebook. Second, many students are in the process of forming their self-concept or self-worth. One low grade may not make that much difference to their self-esteem. However, a pattern of low grades on their assessments resulting in a low final grade during summative assessment speaks volumes.

Howard Gardner, who is a psychologist, former Harvard University professor, and Hobbs Professor of Cognition and Education, wrote a book in 1983 called *Frames of Mind*. From this book came the theory of multiple intelligences, which has influenced teaching and learning since its inception. Gardner's premise is that there is more than one way of knowing things or of being smart. Originally, there were seven such intelligences. Then an eighth, *naturalist*, and a ninth, *existential*, were added. Since these are not new, this book will provide a brief review of these nine intelligences as they relate to teaching and learning in school and in life.

Bodily-Kinesthetic Intelligence (Body Smart)

Bodily-kinesthetic intelligence involves a person's ability to manipulate objects and demonstrate a plethora of different physical skills. It also involves perfecting those skills through the union of mind and body and a unique sense of effective timing. People with a well-developed sense of this intelligence may become dancers, athletes, surgeons, and craftspeople. I am a big sports enthusiast, and when I am watching the sporting events I love, such as baseball, football, tennis, or figure skating, or viewing the Olympics, I am watching athletes with a highly developed sense of bodily-kinesthetic intelligence. However, this intelligence in a classroom can drive some traditional teachers crazy since these students would benefit from being bodily involved in the learning. If a teacher does not provide these opportunities, bodily-kinesthetic students can develop behavior problems. In subsequent chapters, we will discuss how to work movement into your daily lessons so that these students can excel. Babe Ruth, in our assessment, is an example of a person who probably possessed bodily-kinesthetic intelligence.

Interpersonal Intelligence (People Smart)

Interpersonal intelligence is a person's ability to interact effectively with other people. These people can communicate verbally and nonverbally with others, distinguish between the actions and perspectives of others, and are very sensitive to others' moods or temperaments. People with this intelligence often become social workers, actors, and politicians. Students in your classroom with this intelligence become leaders among their peers and, during cooperative learning groups, make great group leaders and facilitators. Two of my three children, Jennifer and Christopher, have a highly developed sense of interpersonal intelligence. Have you noticed that as society becomes more dependent on technology, our students' ability to develop interpersonal intelligence or social skills is becoming severely compromised?

Intrapersonal Intelligence (Self Smart)

I tend to consider this intelligence as the opposite of the one just described. However, I know that a person is capable of having both. Intrapersonal intelligence is a person's ability to understand one's own thoughts and feelings and to use that information in planning and guiding one's own life. These people appreciate not only themselves but the human condition as well. This intelligence is manifested in people who may become psychologists, philosophers, and spiritual leaders. Students in your classroom who exhibit this intelligence may be shy and introverted, but they are very reflective, metacognitive, and self-motivated. In other words, they are always thinking about their own thinking. Journal writing would be a perfect strategy to use with these students. My third child, Jessica, has a highly developed sense of intrapersonal intelligence. Many gifted students do. Bill Gates probably does as well. In my professional life as an educational consultant, I must demonstrate interpersonal intelligence since I am teaching and interacting with educators daily. However, once the workshop has ended, I become very intrapersonal and reflective regarding how the day went and prefer to plan on my own for the next day's effort.

Logical-Mathematical Intelligence (Number/Reasoning Smart)

People who have logical-mathematical intelligence have the ability to calculate, consider hypotheses, and complete mathematical operations. These people can use very abstract, symbolic thought, and inductive and deductive thinking patterns as well as sequential reasoning. Careers that honor this intelligence include mathematicians, scientists, and detectives. Students in your classroom with this intelligence will be attracted to strategic games, math problems, and experiments in science. They will probably score well on the mathematics section of any standardized test, such as the PSAT or SAT, and can be easily assessed on traditional tests. Albert Einstein, on our assessment, probably had logical-mathematical intelligence and, although he initially struggled in school, he made major contributions to society.

Musical Intelligence (Musical Smart)

People who have musical intelligence have the capability to discern rhythm, pitch, tone, and timbre. These people can create, recognize, reproduce, and reflect on music, and there is often a strong connection between music and their emotions. I just described myself. Careers that capitalize on this intelligence are musicians, composers, conductors, vocalists, or just sensitive listeners of music. The logical-mathematical and musical intelligences may share common processes related to thinking. Students in your class who have this intelligence may be constantly singing, rapping, drumming, or beating on their desks and are aware of sounds that other students may not even hear. Having students write a song, rhyme, or rap to symbolize what they are learning is an optimal assessment task for these students. Beethoven more than likely possessed musical intelligence, and we are the better for it.

Linguistic Intelligence (Word Smart)

People who have linguistic intelligence have the ability to use language to express complex meanings. These persons understand the order and meaning of words and can apply *metalinguistic* skills to reflect on the language. This intelligence is obvious in the careers of novelists, poets, journalists, and effective public speakers. Students in your classroom with this type of intelligence enjoy reading, writing, and storytelling. These students probably do well on the verbal sections of standardized tests, such as the PSAT and SAT, and can be easily assessed using traditional tests. Leo Tolstoy, the author of *War and Peace*, probably had linguistic intelligence. How else could he write such a lengthy novel? This is also a strength for me, as a public speaker.

Spatial Intelligence (Picture Smart)

People who have spatial intelligence have the ability to think three dimensionally. Capabilities in this area include an active imagination, mental imagery, spatial reasoning, and graphic and artistic skills as well as the manipulation of images. Those who have careers as pilots, sailors, architects, sculptors, and painters may exhibit spatial intelligence. Students with this intelligence are doodling, drawing, or daydreaming while you are teaching. They also enjoy jigsaw puzzles. Disney, Edison, Gates, Otis, Pasteur, and Picasso, on the quiz you took, probably possessed a high degree of spatial intelligence.

When spatial intelligence was being passed out, I was not present in the room. I have great difficulty reading a map and, years ago, when people were manipulating the Rubik's Cube, the only way I could get all of the same colors on the same side was to peel off the stickers. Those of you who are in my age range will certainly understand. Other educators who don't even know what a Rubik's Cube is at this point will respond, *What?*

These were the original seven intelligences. Gardner added two more since the original list was formed. The two additional ones are as follows.

Naturalist Intelligence (Nature Smart)

People who have naturalist intelligence have the human ability to discriminate among plants and animals, and they are sensitive to additional features of the natural world, such as rocks and clouds. People who were farmers, hunters, and gatherers in our evolutionary cycle were of great benefit to us as a people. Today this intelligence continues to be integral to careers such as chef or botanist. Students' naturalist intelligence is often exploited in our society as consumers attempt to discriminate between kinds of clothes, tennis shoes, makeup, and so forth.

My associates and I had been teaching in El Paso, Texas, when four of us returned home on the weekend between two weeks of instruction. One associate, Warren Phillips, stayed and took a weekend field trip to explore the Carlsbad Caverns. Warren's naturalist intelligence made him an exemplary middle school science teacher and the 2004 Disney Middle School Teacher of the Year. Students in your class who have this intelligence will value learning outside the four walls of the classroom.

Existential Intelligence

The last intelligence added and the one we know least about is existential intelligence. People who have this intelligence are sensitive to and capable of tackling deep questions regarding human existence, such as, *What is the meaning of life? How did we get here? Why do we have to die?* When you have given your objective for the day and a student asks you, *Why do we have to learn this?* he or she is asking an existential question. It really means that the student does not see the connection between what he or she is learning in school and life in the real world. After all, we had brains in the real world long before there was a formal place called school.

If you consider only the first eight intelligences, what percent of these is best assessed through traditional tests? If you said approximately 25 percent, you would be in line with my thinking. Logical-mathematical and linguistic are the two intelligences that have always been assessed on standardized measures of achievement. The other six are more difficult to assess and, therefore, have been devalued in many schools and school systems across the country. If we take out these six, however, we are discounting a sizeable percentage of the talents of students in your classroom, and we may never really know if many students have learned what we have attempted to teach.

The SCANS Report

Supporting evidence for the use of a variety of assessment types also comes from a document known as the SCANS report. In April 1991, then-president George H. W. Bush commissioned a group of experts to determine what skills and abilities would be necessary for high school students to experience success once they entered the workplace in the year 2000. This information became known as the US Secretary's Commission on Achieving Necessary Skills (SCANS) report, and the skills and abilities were categorized into three fundamental skills and five workplace competencies.

Your initial thoughts may be that this information must be outdated since we have been well into the 21st century for some time now. Well, you might want to reconsider in light of two scenarios that have happened since that report was published, confirming that indeed this information is still applicable.

While working for a major school district in Georgia, I was asked by our board of education to assist in planning the agenda for a conference the system was sponsoring for school superintendents throughout the nation. One activity on the agenda was a panel discussion among some of the CEOs of major corporations in Atlanta regarding what they value in hiring current and future employees. We wanted superintendents to hear from those in the trenches about what needed to be done to prepare the students in their districts for the world of work. The panel was comprised of the CEOs of Coca-Cola, Cable News Network (CNN), Emory Healthcare, Georgia Power, and so forth. What they said will be revealed in the paragraphs that follow, since those same skills and competencies were already delineated on the SCANS report. In addition, my daughter Jessica received a job promotion recently and had to demonstrate during the application process at least six of the eight skills and competencies described on the SCANS report.

The sixty-one-page report outlined both the following required fundamental skills and the five workplace competencies.

Fundamental Skills: A Three-Part Foundation

1. Basic Skills: A person's ability to read, write, listen, speak, and perform arithmetic and mathematical operations

2. Thinking Skills: A person's ability to make decisions, problem solve and reason, visualize, think creatively, and know how one learns

3. Personal Qualities: A person's ability to exert a high level of responsibility, self-manage and set personal goals, display sociability and empathy for others, believe in one's own worth, and demonstrate a high level of integrity and honesty

Five Workplace Competencies

1. Resources: A person's ability to identify, organize, plan, and allocate the resources of time, money, material and facilities, and people

2. Interpersonal: A person's ability to participate as a member of a team of men and women from diverse backgrounds, including teaching others new skills, servicing clients or customers, and negotiating and exercising leadership

3. Information: A person's ability to acquire, organize, maintain, interpret, communicate, and evaluate information and use computers to process that information

4. Systems: A person's ability to understand how social, organizational, and technological systems work; operate effectively within and seek to improve or design those systems; and monitor and correct performance

5. Technology: A person's ability to select, apply, maintain, and troubleshoot equipment, including computers and other technologies

Allow me to tell you a personal story that illustrates the importance of these workplace competencies and skills. When I became the executive director of professional development for the school district, there was a secretary in the department who could select any appropriate technology and apply it to the task at hand. However, her ability to service clients and customers left a lot to be desired. In fact, she was so abrupt when answering the telephone that many frustrated callers ended up asking to speak to her boss to complain. I was her boss! I spent so much of my time smoothing ruffled feathers and attempting to maintain the positive reputation that the department had enjoyed for so long that it left little time for me to visualize where the department needed to be and to engage in systems thinking.

I conducted one-on-one conversations with her about her negative attitude, she attended seminars on the topic of customer service, and we wrote a professional development plan together with ways to improve performance. Very little, if anything, changed!

I happen to believe in the power of prayer. I had to place this problem into the hands of a higher power. It worked! She became pregnant! I was so elated that I wanted to send her husband some flowers. I strongly encouraged her to stay at home with her baby, which she was leaning toward doing anyway. When she left, we interviewed prospective applicants for her job. What do you suppose was most important to us as a department—knowledge of technology or interpersonal skills? You guessed it!

From the moment we hired her replacement until the day I retired from the department, which was eight years later, we never had another complaint from a teacher or administrator regarding the secretary who displayed no telephone courtesy. This freed me to be able to do my job as the leader of an award-winning department. Did our new hire know everything she needed to know about the technologies required for the job? No, but she attended classes and quickly acquired the necessary workplace technological competencies. There is a moral to this story. In my educational career, I have discovered that it is much easier to teach the variety of technologies needed for a job than to teach a person interpersonal skills when they have none.

Examine the list from the SCANS report. What percentage of these eight skills and competencies is best assessed with traditional tests? If you said approximately 25 percent, you guessed right again (perhaps it's only basic skills and thinking skills). Even the allocation of resources requires a more constructed response than a true/false or matching task would provide. Then tell me why schools spend so much time assessing only 25 percent of what students should know and be able to do if they are to be career ready. I know one reason: those two skills and competencies are easier to grade.

Answer to Question 2

What evidence supports the use of a variety of assessment types?

There are two theories and one report that support the need for a variety of assessment types in order for all students to excel. The theory of left and right hemisphericity points to the fact that, while people may have preferences, teachers should be teaching to and using assessment types that address both hemispheres of the brain. The theory of multiple intelligences notes various ways to know things, and yet only about 25 percent of those ways are best assessed through traditional measures. The SCANS report outlines three fundamental skills and five workplace competencies that high school graduates should demonstrate if they are to be career ready. Only about 25 percent of these skills and competencies are best measured through traditional assessments. The goal of all educational pursuits is for students to achieve success in school and in life. Therefore, educators would do well to remember this information that supports the use of a variety of instructional strategies as well as assessment types.

How Can I Create a Brain-Compatible Classroom Environment That Fosters High Academic Achievement?

You can do everything within your power to teach the required standards or objectives on which your students will be tested. But unless your classroom is a brain-compatible one that fosters success, your students may not do as well on tests as you might expect. The following are six assumptions about the brain that should be considered if teachers are to create brain-compatible classroom environments that help to ensure student success.

Brain Assumption 1: Neurons That Fire Together, Wire Together

(Jensen and Dabney, 2000; Medina, 2008)

A teacher once told me, "I don't repeat myself in class! If they don't get it the first time, that's simply too bad!" I calmly replied to her, "If you don't repeat yourself, then you don't expect most students to remember."

According to educational consultant Eric Jensen (2000), a pioneer in brain research, recall and meaning are enhanced by mental practice, rehearsal, and repetition. Most brains need to hear something a minimum of three times before the information begins to stick. In fact, John Medina (2008), molecular biologist and author of the best seller *Brain Rules*, states that persons can improve their chances of remembering something if the environment in which the information was initially put into the brain is replicated.

Here is an example to which you may be able to relate. Has anyone ever called your cell phone and left a message with a phone number because you were not available? Have you ever had to play the message back more than once to get the telephone number? Sometimes you have to replay the message at least twice. I am convinced that in fairy tales, this is the reason for *three* bears, *three* little pigs, and *three* billy goats.

Teachers should not even consider assessing a concept unless it has been taught once and reviewed at least twice. Why? As concepts are learned, messages in the brain are passed from one neuron, or specialized memory cell, to another across a space or gap, called the synapse. Messages traveling from one neuron to the next have to cross this gap in order for the signal to continue along its path. A single neuron is capable of receiving messages from several thousand different cells simultaneously. Every time a student reviews the content you teach, the neuronal connection is strengthened. When it comes time for the student to recall the concept for a test, he or she can recall the concept that has been taught and reviewed numerous times rather than one that is recently learned.

This is also the reason that math teachers should not assign twenty-five or thirty math problems for homework. When students are unsure of a process for solving a problem, they may solve the problem incorrectly. Those neuronal connections are strengthened in error, and it will take many additional practices to rewire the brain to the correct procedure. Three to five problems will indicate to a teacher whether a student has acquired the skills or strategies necessary for solving the problem. Feedback should be provided and three to five more problems given if additional practice is needed.

When we prepare students to take tests, we want their brains to fire on all cylinders. While research (Hattie, 2012) relates that labeling students according to their learning styles does not appear to result in increased academic achievement, brain research suggests that with the use of the visual, auditory, kinesthetic, and tactile modalities, which teachers can access when presenting or reviewing content, it is easier for all students to access those connections on test day. Chapters 7, 8, and 9 will provide a plethora of ways teachers can address multiple modalities while assessing.

Brain Assumption 2: The Brain Reacts Negatively to High Stress or Threat

(Willis, 2006; Fogarty, 2009)

I have observed frustrated teachers who impress upon students the importance of doing well on upcoming standardized or criterion-referenced tests. Shouts of "If you don't pass this test, you're staying back in the third grade" or "You must get a very high SAT score to qualify for admission into the college you have chosen" can be heard resounding in the halls and classrooms of schools throughout the United States. I have even seen kindergarten students crying because so much pressure is put on them to do well on test day. When I witness these scenarios, I think to myself, *Teacher, you may have just negatively affected the amount of information these students will be able to recall when the time for the test arrives.* According to neurologist and classroom teacher Judy Willis (2006), stress, anxiety, boredom, and alienation that students can experience in class block the transmission of neurons, connections of synapses, and growth of dendrites, all of which manifest when students are learning.

Here is a personal story. My daughter Jennifer was an excellent, hardworking student in college. As an education major, she earned high grades and was very well prepared to enter the teaching profession upon graduation. During her student teaching experience, she was assigned to a wonderfully engaging educator who used brain-compatible strategies to deliver instruction. However, Jennifer did not have much confidence in her test-taking ability. When it came time to take the Praxis, a comprehensive exam required for those entering the teaching profession, she was scared to death. Jennifer called me on Monday and proclaimed that she was fearful of not passing the Praxis exam, which she was scheduled to take the following Saturday. From what I know about the brain, I realized that I would have to find a way to change that perception if she was going to have any chance of passing this all-important exam. I reminded Jen of her excellent preparation during her coursework; I even helped her visualize herself walking into the testing room and *knocking the top off* the test. I might not have gotten through to her, but I had a few more days to try. On Wednesday, I called her to see how she was feeling. Her tone was a bit more optimistic, so we repeated the affirmations and visualizations. I also reminded her how hard she had worked and how capable she was of doing well. By Friday, I sensed a definite difference in her attitude. I told her I loved her and wished her well! On Saturday, she took the test and passed with flying colors. If she had taken that same test on Monday, I really don't think she would have passed. Keep in mind that she didn't know any more information on Saturday than she did on Monday. It was her attitude and confidence in her ability that made the discernible difference!

You see, the cognitive brain of the student is able to process when students feel safe. When students are faced with fear, anxiety, and threat, the emotional part of the brain takes over (Fogarty, 2009). In fact, blood leaves the frontal lobe, where higher-level thinking occurs, and shifts downward into the survival part of the brain. I even tell parents in my workshops that the worst possible time to discipline their children is when their brains are in a high state of stress or anger. That is when parents are more prone to abuse.

A student's confidence is not easy to observe in a classroom. However, a display of confidence is very easy to observe when watching sports. A baseball player who gets a hit during one at-bat will often get another hit during the next at-bat. A field-goal kicker who makes one field goal has a better chance of kicking the next field goal through the goalposts. Regardless of the sport, listen to the number of times the announcer uses the word *confidence* to describe the attitude of a winning athlete. On the contrary, an athlete who drops a ball or makes an error will often make another error. Tiger Woods is an example of a loss in confidence. While he was once the number one golfer in the world, he now has difficulty finishing in the top ten of a golf tournament. Tiger has not lost his ability to play golf; he has lost his confidence in his ability to play golf. Oftentimes, you will see the level of confidence change from one team to another during a game. This is known as a *momentum shift*, which can often result in a change in the existing score. Regardless of how you personally feel about the standardized, criterion-referenced, or end-of-course tests students are required to take, allow students to approach these tests with a positive attitude and confidence in their abilities to do well. One teacher related to me that on days when her students take tests, those tests are referred to as *celebrations*, not tests, since the tests give students an opportunity to celebrate the learning by showing what they know!

Test day is not the time for the teacher to play "Taps" as students enter the classroom. For over ten years, my daughter Jennifer, who, by the way, has made a wonderful teacher (just as I expected), has played "We Will Rock You," by Queen, to give students the confidence to believe that they can actually *rock the test*. Funny! Although teaching in a Title I school, where the percentage of students who received free or reduced lunch was very high, every year her students had some of the highest second- and third-grade test scores in the building. Now she is an academic coach and assists other teachers in achieving those same results.

Brain Assumption 3: True Learning Occurs When Both Hemispheres of the Brain Are Engaged

(Jensen, 2008; Medina, 2008)

In chapter 2, one of the research theories espoused was one regarding left and right hemisphericity. The conclusion was that, even though there may be preferences, the brains of today's students are using both left and right hemispheres while learning. Since we are actually all whole brained, every area of the brain determines what is needed and interacts with other areas to perform (Jensen, 2008). Therefore, while teaching, teachers must use instructional strategies that honor both hemispheres if they want students to learn the content they are teaching. According to Medina (2008), "the right side of the brain tends to remember the gist of an experience, and the left brain tends to remember the details" (p. 250). Left-hemisphere strategies appear to assist students in doing well in school, while right-hemisphere strategies appear to assist students in doing well in real life. Is it not the job of every teacher to help ensure that they do well in both?

Did you know that countries in the world that have some of the highest test scores in math and science also have some of the strongest music and art programs? Yet, in many school systems across the nation, art and music programs are being eliminated since they are not seen as direct contributors to students' academic achievement. The good news is that teachers in other parts of the country are realizing the importance of the math/music connection in students' brains, and schools are adding the art component to math, science, and technology programs, so the acronym STEM now becomes STEAM (science, technology, engineering, art, and math). The beauty of the instructional strategies outlined in this book is that they all make learning more memorable for both hemispheres of the brain.

What, then, does this information have to do with test performance? Since a preponderance of students with strengths in either left or right hemispheres sits in every classroom, teachers would do well to include assessment options for both hemispheres if they really want to know whether students are truly learning. Traditional selected-response test items are probably more in line with characteristics of the left hemisphere. Remember that my daughter Jessica, the gifted Anna Marie in our story, appears to score higher and prefers those types of test items to show what she knows. Authentic, constructed-response test items, where students are assessed through the products they create or the performances they demonstrate, are more indicative of right-hemisphere characteristics. Remember that my son, Chris, on the other hand, better demonstrates what he knows when he is writing a song, drawing a picture, or acting out a scene from history. If a teacher does not utilize both types of assessments, neither my son nor my daughter will truly be able to show what he or she has learned.

Brain Assumption 4: Learning Is *State* Dependent
(Goleman, 1992; Hattie, 2009)

I advocate that teachers stand at the door and greet students every day when students arrive at school or when changing classes. There are several benefits to this practice. First of all, it is the beginning of the relationship between the teacher and the student. Relationships are everything! According to multiple research studies, teachers who use particular teaching methods, have high expectations for all students, and create positive student-teacher relationships are more likely to have above-average effects on student achievement (Hattie, 2009). Second, while greeting students and watching their facial expressions, a teacher can tell the initial state of each student's brain. If a student has had an argument with a parent before leaving home or a quarrel with a girlfriend or boyfriend in the hall prior to coming to class, the state of his or her brain will be affected.

A state is a mood, or temporary condition, of the brain. The ideal state of the brain during testing is a state of *relaxed alertness*. That term sounds like an oxymoron. It is not! In this state, performance demands on students are increased, but they still consider themselves capable of meeting those demands. According to Goleman (1992), flow occurs in the delicate balance between boredom and anxiety. A student who is not relaxed could be in too high of a state of stress to do well on test day. That condition is not good! A student with no stress about the test or anything else could not care less and will often walk in, put his or her head on the desk, and may even go to sleep. That is equally as bad! When watching sporting events, I find that the athletes who perform best are the ones whose stress level is low to medium and confidence level is high. I desire this same state for my students on the day that they must take any test.

Brain Assumption 5: It Is Easier to Retrieve *Episodic Memories*

(Jensen, 2008; Sprenger, 2007)

In most classes, teachers attempt to put information into one of the weakest memory systems in the human brain. The system is called *semantic memory*, and it involves our ability to recall facts, people's names, and the dates on which things happen. This is the reason why I never have participants in my workshops stand and introduce themselves at the beginning of class. If you did not know their names when you arrived, you still will not know their names when the activity is completed. It is a waste of instructional time. Semantic memory is also the reason a person can cram for an exam and not remember a blessed thing once the exam has ended.

Another memory system supports semantic memory. It is called *episodic memory*. Episodic memory involves the circumstances and locations that accompany our memories. According to Jensen (2008), episodic memory is easily formed and updated and requires little effort or practice. In class, episodic memory involves the sights, sounds, smells, and tastes of learning. This includes where the student sat when learning or attempting to recall the information as well as where the teacher stood when the concept was taught. It also encompasses those visuals on the wall, peripheral and otherwise, which can be so crucial to memory.

Let me see if this story will make this concept clearer. I was teaching a workshop years ago at Wiley High School in Wiley, Texas. I was to teach the same teachers all week. Therefore, on Monday, I asked my participants to give me a specific way to remember their first names so that I could call them by name for the remainder of the week. That was more than fifteen years ago, and I still remember their names. One teacher's name was Rosemary, and she told me that I would see her face in the spice rack in my home. She was right! Whenever I look at the rosemary in my spice rack, I still see her face. A different teacher had a long, blond ponytail that flowed down her back. When she introduced herself to the class, she folded her arms, shook her head once, and replied, "My name is Jeannie!" To those of you who are in my age range, you will, no doubt, remember the television show *I Dream of Jeannie* and how she engaged in the same behavior whenever she granted a wish. It was one of my favorite shows. All day Monday, I called Jeannie by name.

Tuesday came and I could not locate Jeannie in class. What do you suppose had happened? Jeannie had changed her clothes and had taken down her ponytail. She also changed the location of her seat in class. When Jeannie changed her appearance and seat, she was disrupting my *episodic memory*. These memories were tied directly to my memory of her name, which was in *semantic memory*.

It is preferable for students to be in the same environment during testing that they were in when the content was taught. In this way, students not only recall what they have learned but also the conditions (locations and circumstances) of the learning. However, we know this is not always possible. High school students certainly cannot take the PSAT or SAT in the same rooms where they learned the information that they are attempting to recall while taking those tests.

Teachers also complain to me that they are often asked to take down the visuals on the wall related to the test their students are taking. I tell them not to worry! If those visuals have been on the wall long enough, they are housed in the *episodic memories* of students and can be visualized when students are trying to recall the information during testing.

Even better news is that two additional memory systems in the brain are much stronger than semantic or episodic memories. They are procedural (or muscle) memory and reflexive memory. Procedural memory involves the use of the body so that anything a student learns while moving tends to be hardwired into a stronger memory system in the brain. This is why people seldom forget how to drive a car, ride a bike, type, or play the piano. According to Sprenger (2007), a movement repeated often enough becomes a permanent memory.

Reflexive memory involves emotion and is the reason that students will recall information a great deal easier when taking a test if there was an emotional connection to the content when they were learning the information. It is also the reason that students learn more from teachers whom they care about and teachers who care about them.

Brain Assumption 6: Information Is Learned and Remembered Best in a Relevant, Authentic Environment

(Diamond, 1998; Willis, 2006)

The original purpose of the brain was survival in the real world. Wouldn't it make sense that, when teaching the brain, the closer one can get the instruction to what happens in the real world, the more sense it makes?

Marian C. Diamond (1998), professor of anatomy at the University of California, conducted a study in which she placed mice in three different experimental groups and measured the growth of their dendrites, or brain cells. (By the way, every time the brain learns something new, it grows a new dendrite.) The mice in one group were placed in separate cages. There were no wheels to run on, things to do, or other mice with which to communicate. After a certain period, the dendritic growth of their brains was measured. These mice appeared to learn a few things but not many. A second group was placed in cages in pairs and supplied with wheels and manipulatives. I don't know what mice discuss, but at least they could communicate. The dendritic growth of these mice was better than those in group one. The third group of mice was released in a simulated real-world environment. They had to solve problems and find food. In other words, these mice had to operate as they would in the real *mouse* world. You guessed it! The growth of the brain cells in these mice was exponentially greater, leading us to believe that, at least in mice, brains grow better in the real world than in artificial learning environments.

While we should be cautious about generalizing about studies with mice compared to what happens in the human brain, results appear similar when teachers relate concepts in school to those that occur in students' lives. Superior learning actually occurs when stress is lowered and learning is relevant to students' interests, lives, and experiences (Willis, 2006). A question teachers should ask when planning a lesson is, *Where does this concept appear in the lives of my students?* If a teacher does not ask and answer that question, the next existential question will come from the student: *Why do we have to learn this?*

Let's look at several examples of teachers who make content relevant. One teacher told me that he could not get his high school math students to understand the concept of logarithms until the Japanese earthquake happened. He told students who were following that headline that the Richter scale for measuring the intensity of earthquakes is a logarithmic scale. He added that a seven is so, so much more severe than a six on the Richter scale. The light bulb went on in the brains of students, and logarithms began to make sense.

When I teach math, I do not necessarily start with the math problems in the textbook, which have no relevance to most students. I may use those later for practice, but initially I create original math problems within the context of students' lives; I work the names of the students into the problems so that they see themselves solving them. For example, to teach students the concept of elapsed time, we used the daily schedule of a student named Dana. I put her schedule on the board from the time she awakes until the time she goes to bed. I then created problems of elapsed time from one event to the next event in Dana's day. It meant more to the brains of students to work on Dana's day than a word problem in the math textbook.

Traditional, selected-response tests are typically used for summative assessment. However, if we expect students to remember the concept long after the test is over and to apply it in their lives, at some point during instruction and formative assessment, teachers would do well to use relevant examples taken from the lives of their students.

Answer to Question 3

How can I create a brain-compatible classroom environment that fosters high academic achievement?

A brain-compatible classroom environment that fosters high achievement is one where:

- Content is taught and reviewed to strengthen neuronal connections

- The testing environment is viewed positively and students have the confidence to believe they can do well

- Instructional strategies and assessment practices address both left and right hemispheres of the brain

- Students take tests in a state of relaxed alertness

- Students recall information in both semantic and episodic memory systems

- Authentic, real-world examples are used to enable students to remember content long after the tests are over

QUESTION 4

How Can I Begin With the End in Mind?

As I conduct professional learning workshops across the country and encourage educators to actively engage the brains of students, teachers complain to me about the massive amount of content they are expected to teach. While they admit that it is their desire to have a more engaging classroom, they say it is more expedient to conduct a class where they lead rather than facilitate, where they are the *sage on the stage* and not the *guide on the side*. After all, their students often carry textbooks with over five hundred pages. Through lecture, more information can be imparted and more content covered in a shorter amount of time. Remember the thoughts of the renowned educator Madeline Hunter: "If all teachers are doing is covering content, then they should take a shovel and cover that content with dirt since it is dead to memory."

Less Is More

Isn't it ironic that while teaching in Singapore, I noticed that students carried mathematics textbooks about one-third the size of those in the United States? Yet, as a country, these same students scored higher than US students, particularly in the area of math, leading me to believe that *less could actually be more!*

In a 2004 *Educational Leadership* article, the mathematics scope and sequence charts of grades 1–8 from three states in the United States were compared to the scope and sequence of those same grades in three top-achieving countries in the world. The results were eye-opening! In each of the three US states, teachers were required to teach an average of twenty individual math concepts at grade 1 and twenty at grade 2. In each of the top-achieving countries, at grades 1 and 2, only three concepts were addressed: *whole number meaning, whole number operations,* and *measurement units.* Even at grade 8, the average number of US concepts was twenty, while the top-achieving countries never exceeded seventeen. While the number of US concepts remained relatively constant from grades 1 through 8, students in top-achieving countries began with a very limited number of concepts to provide a mathematical foundation, with the number increasing slightly every year until seventeen concepts were reached at grade 8.

Could it be that in many instances, teachers in the United States are teaching horizontally, trying to cover as much content as possible within a specific amount of time, while top-achieving countries are teaching vertically, grouping content into a limited number of segments, or chunks, and delving deeper into each chunk? The Common Core State Standards appear to be a step in the right direction in that the number of standards to be addressed at a grade level is reduced from previous curricula.

It is impossible to give equal treatment to every concept contained in a curriculum guide or textbook while attempting to engage the brains of students—nor should we. The good news is that active teaching involves backward lesson design. Instead of starting with the gargantuan textbook or a favorite lesson or activity, teachers should be starting with the desired student results. These results are defined as success criteria related to the learning intentions of the lesson (Wiggins & McTighe, 2005).

Backward design makes sense when you consider several analogies. How can airline pilots possibly determine and file their flight plans before they have first determined their destinations? As a presenter of *The 7 Habits of Highly Effective People* (Covey, 1996), I teach Habit 2, which is *Begin with the end in mind.* I have learned through life lessons as I approach any task to visualize what I hope to accomplish by the end of the task in order to know how to begin it. How many times have you attended a faculty meeting and left not knowing exactly why you were there?

As executive director of professional development for a large school district, each time I planned a staff meeting, I determined what the staff and I needed to know, understand, or be able to do following the meeting. The answers to these questions always set the meeting agenda and helped to ensure that the agenda was accomplished. This is also the way I have planned any professional development course or workshop that I have taught through the years. Educators and parents leave these workshops realizing just how much they have learned and feeling that the time was well spent! This is even the way our family plans vacations. Plan your lessons the same way, and your possibility of success increases.

What's Your Purpose?

Purpose is an existential part of life and living that applies to students and adults as well. In fact, I teach that when adults have lost their life's purpose, they tend not to live very long. This may be the reason that Charles Schulz, the *Peanuts* cartoonist, died on the day his last cartoon appeared in the paper. Mr. Rogers died not long after his show went off the air. Joe Paterno died only two months after he was fired as the coach of Penn State's football team. Even with older couples, when one dies, without a purpose, the other may not live very long either. Johnny Cash probably would have lived a great deal longer if June Carter, his wife, had not died first.

Purpose is also a part of the classroom. In order for students to buy into your lesson, students need to understand the lesson's purpose. Oftentimes a teacher will comment, "You need to learn this because it is going to be on the test." That statement may motivate some students, the same ones who ask, "Is this going to be on the test?" But other students couldn't care less! In fact, when students do not see the purpose of your lesson, they will ask the existential question, "Why do we have to learn this?"

Before beginning to plan instruction, teachers need to know what students should know, understand, and be able to do by the end of the lesson. They must also identify the type of evidence they will accept, to confirm that students have truly understood the knowledge or concepts being taught. In the book *Classroom Instruction That Works*, Dean et al. (2012) provide the following four recommendations when setting learning objectives that actually improve student achievement:

1. Be specific but not restrictive.
2. Let students and parents know what the objectives are.
3. Connect the current objectives to those taught previously and those that will be taught in the future.
4. Allow students to set their own personal objectives.

Be Specific But Not Restrictive

Teachers have to know the specific standards, benchmarks, and objectives that students in their school system are required to learn. When those standards are written in terms that are too broad, teachers have to *unpack* those standards and dissect them until they reach specific statements of the knowledge and skills that should be taught. From those statements, teachers can then develop their lesson objectives. These objectives should not be so specific that teachers are unable to provide for the differing needs of students or be so broad that they have little or no meaning. Lesson objectives should be stated in terms of what students are supposed to learn or understand, and not describe an activity in which students are supposed to engage. For example, *Students will solve multiple-step word problems* is a mathematics objective. *Students will complete the even-numbered multiple-step word problems on pages 181–182* is an activity.

Let Students and Parents Know What the Objectives Are

When I was in school, I spent a great deal of time attempting to guess what content that had been taught was actually going to end up on the test. If I guessed correctly, I made a good grade. Now the prevailing thought is to tell students what you expect them to know and be able to do long before the tests ever take place. There should be no surprises!

Learning objectives should be communicated to students both verbally and in writing in language that they can understand. In fact, the purpose of backward design is to enable students to learn the skills necessary for teaching themselves and to regulate their own learning (Hattie, 2009). Parents are also more engaged when they understand what their children are supposed to be learning. Subsequent chapters in this book will deal with the feedback that students should receive so that they can personally know how they are doing.

Connect the Current Objectives to Those Taught Previously and Those That Will Be Taught in the Future

Try this on a member of your family. Ask him to spell the word *shop* out loud. (*S-H-O-P*.) Ask him to spell it again. (*S-H-O-P*.) Ask him to spell it a third time. (*S-H-O-P*.) Now, quickly ask him this question: "What do you do when you get to a green light?" Your family member will probably say, "Stop!" Yet, when we get to a green light, we should *go*. Why are people more likely to say the word *stop*? The closest connection in the brain between *shop* and *light* is *stop*. The brain is always searching for the connections. Teachers need to take advantage of this propensity. It is so much easier to remember one concept when teachers can help students connect it to another one that the student already knows.

Making statements like "This objective is similar to one we studied two weeks ago" or "You will see this concept again in an upcoming unit" helps students connect what they are learning today with what they have already learned or what they will be learning in the future. Any time a teacher can make those connections relevant by using real-life examples, the benefit is more than doubled.

Allow Students to Set Their Own Personal Objectives

Districts across the United States have mandated that teachers post the learning objective and articulate it to students at the beginning of the lesson. However, in many classes, that is the end of any reference to the objective during the entire lesson. Dylan Wiliam (2011) relates that it can be a valuable process for teacher and students to develop the learning objectives jointly. He refers to the process as *co-construction*, which is grounded in the fact that students are more likely to apply learning intentions and criteria for success that they discussed and helped create than those given to them by the teacher.

Although these learning objectives are determined prior to planning the lesson, it may not always be necessary to tell students exactly what the objective of the lesson is. Perhaps some objectives just need to be discovered. Wiliam (2011) relates that "telling the students where they are going could completely spoil the journey!" (p. 57).

Planning the Lesson

I have developed a lesson plan template that helps teachers accomplish this backward lesson design during the planning process by asking and answering questions. Is it necessary for teachers to write out the answers to each of the questions on the template? No! It is necessary, however, that they plan to ask and honestly answer each of the questions. For an in-depth explanation of this plan, consult the references section of *Worksheets Don't Grow Dendrites: 20 Instructional Strategies That Engage the Brain*, 3rd ed. (Tate, 2016). This plan assists teachers in answering the five essential questions that help to ensure planning of a brain-compatible lesson, which will result in high test scores and increased academic achievement. The following sections discuss the five questions for backward lesson design.

Lesson Objective: What Do You Want Students to Know, Understand, and Be Able to Do?

The first of the five questions is the most important since it informs all stakeholders—the teacher, students, and parents—exactly what the expectations are. It determines the learning objective, written in *kid-friendly* terms that everyone can understand, that guides the remainder of the lesson.

Assessment (Traditional/Authentic): How Will You Know That Students Have Mastered Learning?

There is a simpler way to say this. *How will you know when your students know?* In other words, what formative and summative assessment results will allow you to know whether each student has met the lesson's objective and, if not, what needs to happen to make it so? Be certain that you include both traditional and authentic assessment types. Traditional, because these types prepare students for the selected-response format of many of the summative assessments and enable them to be college ready. Authentic, because these types require students to think at higher levels and complete more constructed-response tasks that prepare them to be career ready.

Ways to Gain and Maintain Attention: How Will You Gain and Maintain Students' Attention?

Due to the enormous amount of stimuli in the environment, students' brains cannot pay attention to everything going on around them. Therefore, students must choose whether to attend to your lesson, talk to the peer sitting next to them, or attempt to sneak a text message while you are not looking. Students can even be perfectly still and obviously quiet and pay no attention to your lesson!

A structure in the brain called the hippocampus helps to determine whether today's lesson will be remembered tomorrow. Since the brain does not like clutter, if a student's hippocampus determines that the lesson is not worth remembering, much of the content may be discarded when students go to sleep.

There are four ways to increase the likelihood that students will pay attention and remember content both before and after tests. They are *need, novelty, meaning,* or *emotion*. Note the word *or*, which means that teachers do not have to use all four ways to gain students' attention. I have seen excellent lessons taught while utilizing only one.

The first way to gain students' attention is *need*. People tend to remember things that they perceive they need to know. As the world becomes more technologically advanced and information more easily accessible than ever, we remember fewer and fewer bits of information. Yet, students simply *need* to know such things as the phone numbers of loved ones, in case our cell phones become disabled.

The brain notices things in the environment that are *novel*—new or different. When the same teaching techniques, such as lectures or worksheets, are used daily, students may stop paying attention after a while. This is similar to the way, as a frequent flier, I pay little to no attention to the flight attendant when the instructions are given—unless the attendant uses humor, music, or another novel strategy to present the information. By the way, if you have flown lately, you may notice that both Delta and Southwest Airlines have become wise to the importance of novelty.

To make the content *meaningful*, find a way to connect it to students' lives. This is the same as making the content relevant so that students remember concepts, not only for tests but also for life in the real world.

Of the four ways to gain the student's attention, the most powerful one is *emotion*. Visualize an emotional event that happened in the world (such as the *Challenger* explosion or September 11, 2001) or even one in your personal life. No doubt, you will be able to recall exactly the circumstances of where you were when it happened. Teach students with passion and enthusiasm, emotionally connect them to the content, show them you are concerned for their welfare, and watch their memory of your content increase!

Content Chunks: How Will You Divide and Teach the Content to Engage Students' Brains?

Realizing that even the adult brain can hold only a limited number of isolated bits of information simultaneously (a range of five to nine, with seven being the average), teachers should take the content and break it up into manageable learning segments, or chunks. An activity should be integrated into each chunk to give students' brains time to process the information contained in the chunk. The size of a chunk for a special education student might be different from that of a gifted student. It is dependent on how much students' brains can hold at one time. The following twenty brain-compatible strategies provide the activity inherent in each chunk.

Brain-Compatible Strategies: Which Will You Use to Deliver Content?

Whether you examine Howard Gardner's theory of multiple intelligences discussed in chapter 2 or read any of the books on brain theory, you will realize that teachers should be delivering instruction in twenty ways. These twenty strategies are advantageous since they:

- Teach to both hemispheres of the brain

- Address all of the multiple intelligences

- Engage all four of the learning modalities (visual, auditory, kinesthetic, tactile)

- Can be used with all grade levels (pre-K through adult)

- Can be used with any curricular area

- Increase academic achievement

- Decrease behavior problems

- Make teaching and learning so much fun

Table 4.1 delineates the twenty strategies and correlates them to eight of Gardner's intelligences and to the four learning modalities. While it is not necessary to determine a student's dominant intelligence or modality, teaching to students' strengths and strengthening their weaknesses is a worthwhile endeavor. You may have noticed that many of these strategies have already been used throughout this book to make the content more memorable and easier to understand—storytelling, metaphor, graphic organizers, and visualization, to name only a few. You will also see the strategies reflected in the assessment activities that should be used before, during, and after a lesson.

The lesson plan in figure 4.1 (page 50) is the template that should be used as teachers plan and implement brain-compatible lessons, which help to ensure that students are ready for tests. This plan also assists teachers in knowing whether students retain the information once the test is over. I tell teachers that if they come to question 5 on the lesson plan and cannot check off even one of the twenty strategies, the bad news is that their lesson is not brain compatible and needs to be revisited!

Table 4.1: Comparison of Brain-Compatible Instructional Strategies to Learning Theory

Brain-Compatible Strategies	Multiple Intelligences	Visual, Auditory, Kinesthetic, Tactile (VAKT)
Brainstorming and discussion	Linguistic	Auditory
Drawing and artwork	Spatial	Kinesthetic/tactile
Field trips	Naturalist	Kinesthetic/tactile
Games	Interpersonal	Kinesthetic/tactile
Graphic organizers, semantic maps, and word webs	Logical-mathematical	Visual/tactile
Humor	Linguistic	Auditory
Manipulatives, experiments, labs, and models	Logical-mathematical	Tactile
Metaphors, analogies, and similes	Spatial	Visual/auditory
Mnemonic devices	Musical	Visual/auditory
Movement	Bodily-kinesthetic	Kinesthetic
Music, rhythm, rhyme, and rap	Musical	Auditory
Project-based and problem-based learning	Logical-mathematical	Visual/tactile
Reciprocal teaching and cooperative learning	Linguistic	Auditory
Role-plays, drama, pantomimes, and charades	Bodily-kinesthetic	Kinesthetic
Storytelling	Linguistic	Auditory
Technology	Spatial	Visual/tactile
Visualization and guided imagery	Spatial	Visual
Visuals	Spatial	Visual
Work study and apprenticeships	Interpersonal	Kinesthetic
Writing and journals	Intrapersonal	Visual/tactile

Visit www.learningsciences.com/bookresources for a reproducible version of this table.

Lesson Objective(s): What do you want students to know, understand, and be able to do?

_____

Assessment (Traditional/Authentic): How will you know that students have mastered essential learning?

_____

Ways to Gain/Maintain Attention (Primacy): How will you gain and maintain students' attention? Consider need, novelty, meaning, or emotion.

_____

Content Chunks: How will you divide and teach the content to engage students' brains?

Lesson Segment 1: _____

      Activities: _____

Lesson Segment 2: _____

      Activities: _____

Lesson Segment 3: _____

      Activities: _____

Brain-Compatible Strategies: Which will you use to deliver content?

- ☐ Brainstorming/discussion
- ☐ Drawing/artwork
- ☐ Field trips
- ☐ Games
- ☐ Graphic organizers / semantic maps / word webs
- ☐ Humor
- ☐ Manipulatives/experiments/labs/ models
- ☐ Metaphors/analogies/similies
- ☐ Music/rhythm/rhyme/rap

- ☐ Project/problem-based learning
- ☐ Reciprocal teaching / cooperative learning
- ☐ Role-plays/drama/pantomimes/ charades
- ☐ Storytelling
- ☐ Technology
- ☐ Visualization / guided imagery
- ☐ Visuals
- ☐ Word study / apprenticeship

Figure 4.1: A brain-compatible lesson plan.

Source: Copyright © 2016 by Corwin. All rights reserved. Reprinted from Worksheets Don't Grow Dendrites: 20 Instructional Strategies That Engage the Brain, _3rd Edition, by Marcia L. Tate. Thousand Oaks, CA: Corwin, www.corwin.com._

Visit www.learningsciences.com/bookresources for a reproducible version of this figure.

Hattie (2009) summarizes this chapter succinctly. The emphasis when teaching should be on what students can do, on students knowing what they are supposed to be doing, on using multiple strategies with students for learning how to do, and knowing when students have actually done it. The subsequent chapters in this book will address the multiple strategies that help students know how to do and how teachers will know when students have actually done it.

Answer to Question 4

How can I begin with the end in mind?

When I started to teach over forty years ago, my lesson plans began with what I was planning to teach. I have now learned a more effective way. If teachers determine what students should know, understand, and be able to do, and then plan to make it happen, their mindset is different, and content extraneous to the question's answer is not relevant or important. Knowing this narrows the focus for every lesson. Four additional questions should also be considered when planning a brain-compatible lesson:

1. How will you know that students have mastered essential learning?

2. Will you use need, novelty, meaning, or emotion to gain and maintain students' attention?

3. How many chunks of information do you need to teach, and which activities need to be included in each chunk?

4. Which of the twenty brain-compatible strategies will you use to deliver instruction?

QUESTION 5

How Can I Write Quality Selected- and Constructed-Response Test Items?

Selected-response test items are the most popular types for determining whether students have achieved the desired learning objectives or standards during summative assessment. They are not as compatible for many brains as are constructed-response test items since the latter items are typically closer to what happens in the real world. Selected-response items, however, are also used for creating benchmark tests that measure students' academic progress during formative assessment. Therefore, it would behoove teachers to write the most effective selected-response items that truly measure what all students have learned.

In a selected-response item, students select an answer from choices that have already been determined; they typically include multiple-choice, true/false, and matching tests. Let's begin this chapter by having you take the following test.

A Multiple-Choice Test

1. Which does not belong?

    a. dog

    b. bed

    c. duck

    d. donkey

continued ➡

2. Which does not belong?
    a. 4
    b. 8
    c. 9
    d. 16

The aforementioned items are two to which teachers must respond at the beginning of my assessment workshop. I call on volunteers individually, and they tell me the answer and the rationale for their answer. By now, you have probably figured out that there can be multiple answers to each question. For example, in question 1, the answer could be b) *bed* because it is the only word that starts with a *b*. But it could also be c) *duck* because it is the only answer with two legs, while the others have four. The answer could also be d) *donkey* because it is the only one that is a two-syllable word, while the others are one syllable. For question 2, the answer could be d) *16* because it is the only number that is two digits, or it could be b) *8* because it is the only number that is not a perfect square. I even had one teacher reply that the answer to number 2 is b) *8* because it is the only number word that begins with a vowel while the other number words begin with consonants. Smart thinking!

I then ask participants to reflect with their partners on what this activity actually teaches. Answers vary, but the gist is that there can be reasonable, legitimate rationales for several different answers to a multiple-choice question. Yet, if the answer key considers only one answer as the appropriate choice, all other answers are marked incorrect and the total score is negatively affected. Major decisions are made daily about students based on assessment data and, whether we like it or not, students view those assessment results as tangible, visible evidence of their worth and value.

Whether teachers choose selected-response items or constructed-response items depends on the purpose of the assessment. If the purpose is to measure students' concrete knowledge, selected-response items will suffice. Marzano (2010) refers to these selected-response assessments as one type of obtrusive assessment since all instruction stops during their administration. However, if the purpose is to ascertain qualitative feedback, such as a student's ability to solve a problem or write an essay, a constructed-response item, such as a short answer or essay, would be more appropriate. Teachers must decide when to use either selected- or constructed-response items to determine if students are really learning.

Selected-Response Items

Haladyna (1997) points out the pros and cons of the selected-response format.

Pros

- Students can answer more selected-response questions than constructed-response questions in the same amount of time.

- Student responses can be scored more accurately and more rapidly.

- Multiple-choice questions tend to produce higher reliability and consistency over time.

- The format of these questions is similar to the ones students will encounter on most standardized tests.

- The time and effort spent writing and scoring test items is more efficient.

- Scoring selected-response items can be more objective, while scoring constructed-response items is more subjective (particularly when the items are scored by a variety of people).

- Test results can be compared among students and classes.

- Selected-response questions can be written to assess students' higher-level thinking, just as constructed-response questions can be.

- When written effectively, selected-response tests can provide feedback regarding students' strengths and weaknesses during the formative assessment process.

Cons

- Questions might be written to assess lower-level knowledge only.

- Items are not appropriate for some purposes, such as having students demonstrate their creativity.

- Items do not enable all students to show evidence of their varied multiple intelligences and learning styles.

- Items can be answered correctly by guessing and may not show evidence of true student knowledge, understanding, and reasoning.

- Items will lack evidence of student writing.

If selected-response items are used to determine whether students are really learning, we owe it to students to make those items as valid and reliable as possible.

Multiple Choice

Multiple-choice test items represent the most common type of question on state and national standardized tests. They provide students with a series of answers (usually four) from which students must select the correct one. The following criteria may enable teachers to write multiple-choice items that are more appropriate.

- The level of difficulty of the passages and answer choices should be written on the instructional reading level of the students.

- The central or main idea should be clearly stated in the stem of the question.

- There should clearly be only one best answer.

- The form and grammar of all responses should be consistent, with specific determiners (e.g., *a, an*) avoided if possible.

- Answer choices should be grammatically parallel.

- All distractors should be believable.

- All answer options should be consistent, with no one option being extremely short or long when compared to others.

- Each item should be independent of every other item (i.e., answering an item correctly should not depend on having correctly answered a previous item).

- Direct questions should be used more often than incomplete statement items.

Sample Multiple-Choice Item

Which part of the neuron transmits information to other cells?

    a. dendrites

    b. axon

    c. cell body

    d. synapse

True/False

True/false items are used primarily to assess students' factual knowledge and require students to determine whether a statement is accurate or inaccurate. One major disadvantage of this type of test item is that students have a 50 percent chance of getting the right answer, even if they have no knowledge of the statement. Oftentimes, true/false tests are made more effective if students are asked to provide the correct answer for any statement that is chosen as false. The following criteria may enable teachers to write true/false items that are more appropriate.

- There should be a reasonable number of test items.

- Test items should be clearly true or false.

- Language taken verbatim from the textbook should be avoided.

- Statements that signify opinions should be avoided.

- Negatives in the statement should be avoided.

- Quantitative terms (e.g., *seven principles of government*) rather than qualitative terms (e.g., *several principles of government*) should be used.

- Students should be asked to write the words *true* or *false* rather than *T* or *F* so that no answer can be misinterpreted.

- Answers that are *false* should be corrected to be made *true*.

Sample True/False Item

Write *True* or *False* on the line provided.

_____ Students' attention spans are approximately equal to their ages in minutes.

Matching

Matching test items consists of one column of premises and one column of responses. They require students to connect one item to another to which it is related. Oftentimes, more possible answers exist than items to which they must be matched. The following criteria may enable teachers to write matching items that are more appropriate.

- The lists of items should be brief (five to fifteen).
- The lists should be homogenous.
- All of the answer choices should be on one page.
- Items should be logically ordered.
- Extra answer choices should be included.
- The answer choices should be clear (i.e., either letters, numbers, or words).
- The answer choices should be arranged alphabetically or chronologically, but not mixed or doubled (e.g., *aa, bb*).

Sample Matching Items

Match the following parts of the brain with their descriptions.

A. Improves the ability of axons to carry nervous system signals rapidly
   _____

B. An enlarged area of a neuron containing the nucleus _____

C. The branches on which information is received _____

D. A tail-like structure that transmits information to other cells
   _____

1. cell body

2. myelin

3. axon

4. synapse

5. nucleus

6. neuron

7. dendrites

Fill in the Blank

Fill-in-the-blank items require students to supply a response that fits into a sentence or phrase. These items are not technically selected-response items, since students are not choosing a response, but they require only one correct answer and do not necessitate that students construct a detailed response. The following criteria may enable teachers to write fill-in-the-blank items that are more appropriate.

- A recall format should be used only for the most important information.

- There should be a brief, definitive answer for each item.

- Verbatim textbook language should be avoided.

- The response blanks should be of equal length and not excessive.

- Only the most significant words should be omitted.

- Only one point should be allowed for each blank.

- A scoring key should be prepared that contains all acceptable student answers.

Sample Fill-in-the-Blank Item

All functions of the brain and nervous system are based on communication between nerve cells called _____.

Short Constructed-Response Items

Short constructed-response items require students to construct an answer as opposed to simply selecting one among the answer choices provided; they are therefore more challenging than the previous categories. One advantage of this type of format is that a single constructed-response question can often be used to assess student understanding of several different concepts. However, these items are more difficult to score since a student's answer could range from totally incorrect to totally correct, and every answer in between. When writing short constructed-response items, Ainsworth (2015) delineates the following six item-writing guidelines:

- The item should be a direct question and not an incomplete statement.

- The question should measure an essential aspect of the unit's instructional focus.

- The wording of the question should be clear enough to require an appropriate but brief response.

- If the item requires completion, the response blank should be at the end.

- If there are two response blanks in the question, the blanks should be of equal length so that they do not provide clues.

- Enough space should be provided for a complete student response.

Sample Short Constructed-Response Item

Briefly explain what would happen if a message in the brain failed to cross the synapse.

Extended Constructed-Response Items

When students are asked to write a very detailed answer to a question or prompt, this item is considered to be an extended constructed response and usually appears in the form of an essay. The following criteria may enable teachers to write extended constructed-response items that are more appropriate.

- At least two essay questions should be included so that full or no credit can be avoided.

- Vague, all-encompassing questions should be avoided.

- Higher-order verbs should be used in the stem of the essay question. (Consult chapter 6 for sample higher-order verbs.)

- The length of the student's response should be made clear (e.g., one paragraph, one page).

- Criteria for each question should be clearly defined with a separate point value for each part of the question.

- Open-book essay questions should be avoided. (This type of test actually measures reading speed or study skills. Students who read better than others have a definite advantage.)

- In the case of mathematics, the number of word problems should be limited and an excessive number of problems of the same kind avoided.

- Point values for all questions should be explained or rubrics provided so that students know how to divide their writing time.

- A preliminary teacher outline of all acceptable answers should be constructed for grading purposes.

Sample Extended Constructed-Response Item

Select <u>one</u> of the questions below and write an essay that answers the question.

1. It has been said that the human brain is the most complex structure in the known universe. Why might this statement be true? Include five facts regarding what you have learned in class about the human brain.

2. The human brain is a computer. What are five reasons why this metaphor just may be accurate? Support your reasons with specific facts you have learned about the brain.

Answer to Question 5

How can I write quality selected- and constructed-response test items?

Selected-response test items are perhaps the most popular type to determine whether students have achieved desired learning outcomes. They also prepare students to pass benchmark and summative assessments, are easier to grade, and are more objective. However, the tests' disadvantages include their inability for students to demonstrate their creativity and higher levels of thought. Constructed-response test items are more subjective and more difficult to grade but tend to be closer to those skills that students are actually expected to demonstrate in the real world. When writing both selected- and constructed-response items, consult the test review checklists in this chapter to ensure that the items are more effective for telling whether students are really learning. The checklists can also be shared with students to assist them in writing quality questions for their peers.

How Can Effective Questioning Show That Students Are Learning?

Teachers ask questions daily. With the exception of teacher talk, questioning was the second-most dominant teaching method used in classrooms (van Lier, 1998). Asking appropriate questions is so essential for enabling a teacher to know whether students are truly learning, that this entire chapter is devoted solely to this teaching technique and assessment method.

It is a given that teachers ask questions. What we really want to know is whether teachers are asking the right questions. When asking questions and responding to student answers, give-and-take between teacher and student talk should take place. Research (Hiebert et al., 2003; Wiliam, 2011) shows that significant differences in the proportion of teacher to student talk exist among countries. Much to my surprise, American teachers actually talk less than teachers in higher-achieving countries do. When you examine the results, however, you may realize that it is the quality of the talk, rather than the quantity, that determines how much students are learning (Wiliam, 2011). It then becomes the teacher's job to ensure that the talk that ensues will be of the highest quality.

If students' brains are to be conditioned to think at higher levels, teachers should ask higher-order questions of students. They should do so when using the strategy of brainstorming and discussion and when modeling aloud the thought processes that occur in the brain when those questions are being answered. Higher-order questions appear to be more effective than factual questions since they not only enable teachers to know whether students are learning the actual material but may have a broader general effect on students' understanding of other unrelated material as well. In other words, higher-order questions may help students learn how to learn.

Determiners of Quality Questions

Walsh and Sattes (2005) characterize quality questions in the following ways.

- Quality questions are purposeful.

- Quality questions are clearly focused on content.

- Quality questions engage students at a variety of appropriate cognitive levels.

- Quality questions are clear and concise.

- Quality questions are seldom asked simply by chance.

Quality Questions Are Purposeful

The purpose of the question is dependent on the objective of the lesson and the context in which the question will be asked. Two contexts, according to Walsh and Sattes, are *recitation* and *discussion*. The most common, *recitation*, occurs when a teacher poses a question and, after the student answers, the teacher either affirms or corrects the answer. These questions are typically low level and require that students recall information about the lesson, define a word or concept, or demonstrate their conceptual understanding.

Researcher Brualdi (1998) relates that teachers ask between three and four hundred of these recitation questions daily, with the majority of them falling into the low-level cognitive categories. Approximately 6 percent of the time students are asked to recall information, and 20 percent of the time the questions deal with procedural information (Wilen, 1991). These percentages reflect the belief of many educators that teaching is merely presenting information to be recalled and, therefore, questioning is designed to ascertain whether that information has been remembered (Hattie, 2009).

There is a time and place for recitation questions. These types of questions might be used for the following purposes.

- To find out what students know about a topic

- To see whether students comprehend a passage

- To provide drill and practice of a skill

- To encourage dialogue in cooperative groups

- To check on homework completion and understanding

- To review prior to a test

In a high school social studies lesson I taught, the following recitation question was asked: *What are the first ten amendments to the United States Constitution, also known as the Bill of Rights?*

True *discussion* questions, on the other hand, occur much less frequently. According to Dillon (1984), these questions are asked only about 4 to 8 percent of the time. Discussion questions are usually thought provoking and open ended; additional questions are asked only for clarification. All students are given the opportunity to participate and support their responses with evidence. Students do not have to wait for the teacher's permission to respond or to look to the teacher for affirmation or correction.

Discussion questions may be used for the following purposes.

- To assist students in understanding a topic

- To offer students an opportunity to form hypotheses and provide evidence to support ideas

- To encourage students to listen to and respect the differing ideas of peers

- To help students make connections that will enable them to put information into long-term memory

- To give students opportunities to apply learning to other contexts

A discussion question, rather than one of recitation, for the same aforementioned social studies lesson would have been as follows: *Can you think of a situation in which one of your amendment rights was violated? Explain.*

Quality Questions Are Clearly Focused on Content

During the more than twenty-five years that I have taught teachers, I have learned that one of the teachers' biggest concerns was that each year they are given more and more content to teach but no additional time to teach it. They must consider standardized and criterion-referenced tested objectives and mandated state and national curricular objectives, as well as what students simply need to know or be able to do. *Dr. Tate*, teachers ask, *What do I teach and what can I omit?*

One high school American history teacher told me that he was expected to cover the Vietnam War in *one* class period. My first inclination was to inquire, with astonishment, about how it was humanly possible to accomplish that feat. After all, America's involvement in the Vietnam War lasted for more than ten years. How could this information be condensed into a fifty-five-minute class period?

If you recall the lesson plan template discussed in chapter 4, you remember that it is patterned after Wiggins and McTighe's backward lesson design process: the first question a teacher should ask is, *What do I want students to know, understand, and be able to do?* My response to the American history teacher was as follows. Obviously, you cannot cover the entire Vietnam War in one class period. Therefore, ask yourself this question: *By the end of the period, what do I want my students to know and understand regarding the Vietnam War?* He stated that it made so much more sense to him when he looked at his lesson plan this way. Quality questions must be focused directly on the content to be learned, to be relevant to student understanding.

Quality Questions Engage Students at a Variety of Appropriate Cognitive Levels

Analyzing the types of questions students ask one another is probably more important than the questions teachers ask. Therefore, there is something to be said for teaching students how to ask better questions and then listen to see whether they are doing so (Hattie et al., 1998). This section will be devoted to analyzing several different models of questioning, or levels of tasks that students are asked to accomplish; this helps to ensure that students' thought processes are operating at higher levels.

Bloom's Taxonomy (Revised)

The first model is the revised version of the original Bloom's taxonomy, to which we were all introduced in college education courses. The lower levels of *Remember* and *Understand* are ripe for asking recitation questions, while the upper levels of *Apply*, *Analyze*, *Evaluate*, and *Create* lend themselves to those discussion questions and tasks that engender higher levels of cognition. Figure

6.1 displays the verbs that should be used when asking questions or performing tasks at various levels of the taxonomy.

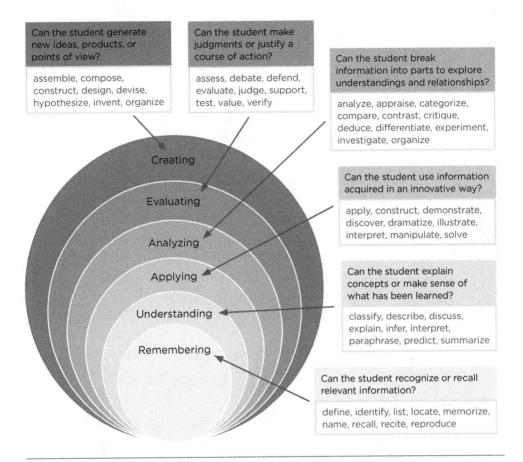

Figure 6.1: Bloom's taxonomy (revised).

The Structure of Observed Learning Outcomes (SOLO) Questioning Taxonomy

A second taxonomy of knowing is the SOLO taxonomy, developed by John Biggs, which constitutes a systematic way of describing how a student's performance develops from simple to complex as it relates to learning. There are five stages reflected on the pyramid in figure 6.2 (page 68): three quantitative phases (*Pre-structural*, *Uni-structural*, and *Multi-structural*) and two qualitative phases (*Relational* and *Extended Abstract*). The verbs displayed can assist teachers in asking questions or involving students in tasks that are multidimensional.

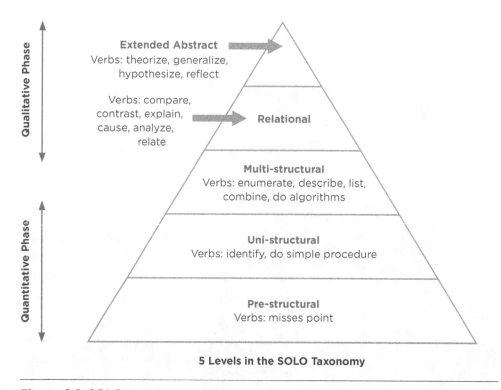

Figure 6.2: SOLO taxonomy.

Source: John B. Biggs & K. Collis; retrieved from www.educatingmatters.wordpress.com.

Depth of Knowledge (DoK)

A third model of questioning or tasks is Norman Webb's (2009) *Depth of Knowledge.* This model classifies tasks according to the level of complex thinking students would have to use to accomplish the tasks successfully. It is organized into four increasingly complex levels.

Level 1: Recall and Reproduction. Requires students to recall facts, apply simple procedures, or remember the correct response. It answers the question, *What is the knowledge?* Verbs: *compute, define, identify, illustrate, list, recall, recognize.*

Level 2: Basic Skills and Concepts. Requires students to make decisions about the appropriate approach to take. It answers the question, *How can the knowledge be used?* Verbs: *categorize, cause/ effect, compare, estimate, organize, predict, summarize.*

Level 3: Strategic Thinking and Reasoning. Requires students to think abstractly and justify their choices among many responses. It answers the question, *Why can the knowledge be used?* Verbs: *assess, critique, draw conclusions, formulate, hypothesize, investigate, solve.*

Level 4: Extended Thinking. Requires students to synthesize information from a variety of sources or to transfer knowledge from one domain to solve real-world problems in another domain. It answers the question, *What else can be done with the knowledge?* Verbs: *analyze, connect, create, critique, design, prove, synthesize.*

Quality Questions Are Clear and Concise

Once the first three characteristics of quality questions have been considered, it is time to formulate the question. Walsh and Sattes (2005) suggest that the question be written and read several times for clarity and be assessed according to the following criteria.

- Do students understand the question such that they can translate it into their own language?

- Will all students understand the type of response the question requires?

- Are questions grammatically correct?

- Do questions address only one issue for response?

- Are students provided with enough contexts to enable them to respond accurately?

Quality Questions Are Seldom Asked Simply by Chance

The more I consider what it takes for teachers to write appropriate higher-level questions, the more I realize how time-consuming this practice can truly be. This is probably the main reason that many teachers fail to invest the time. When teachers realize that only a few carefully developed *pivotal questions* can move students into the major part of the lesson and their thinking to higher levels (Walsh & Sattes, 2005), teachers may come to understand that the time expended is more than worth it. The process will be successfully facilitated if grade-level or content-area teachers work together to create these questions. Once these questions are written, they should be kept from year to year and shared with teachers in other schools who teach the same curriculum.

Sample Cross-Curricular Higher-Order Questions or Tasks

Listed below are sample cross-curricular questions and tasks that can challenge students' brains to think at higher levels. The levels of Bloom's taxonomy, SOLO taxonomy, and Webb's Depth of Knowledge, which each task or question addresses, are indicated in parentheses following the question or task.

English/Language Arts

- Compare and contrast two pieces of literature. (For example: Compare and contrast the fairy tale *Cinderella* and the African folktale *Mufaro's Beautiful Daughters*.) How are they alike? How are they different? (Analyzing, Relational, Basic Skills and Concepts)

- What did the author mean when (s)he wrote . . .? (For example: How does Emily Dickinson depict Death in the poem "I Could Not Stop for Death"?) Cite text evidence. (Understanding, Relational, Strategic Thinking and Reasoning)

- Is the author's statement a fact or an opinion? Explain why. (Understanding, Relational, Strategic Thinking and Reasoning)

- How would you summarize the story or poem that we read? Which major details should be included in your summary and which should not? (Understanding, Relational, Basic Skills and Concepts)

Mathematics

- What is the answer to the following problem? Explain why your answer is the correct one. (Understanding, Relational, Recall and Reproduction)

- What appropriate tools would you use to measure the following objects? (For example: What appropriate tools would you use to measure the width of the top of your desk, your waistline, and the distance from the door of your classroom to the window?) Record the measurements on your paper. (Understanding, Uni-structural, Strategic Thinking and Reasoning)

- Draw and identify geometric shapes. (For example: Draw and identify lines, line segments, rays, angles, and perpendicular and parallel lines.) (Applying, Uni-structural, Recall and Reproduction)

- Which formula should be used to solve the following problem? Why did you select that formula over others? Use the formula to solve the problem. (Applying, Multi-structural, Strategic Thinking and Reasoning)

Science

- Compare and contrast two scientific processes (For example: Compare and contrast mitosis and meiosis.) How are the processes alike, and how are they different? (Analyzing, Relational, Basic Skills and Concepts)

- Is there evidence to support an author's recommendation for solving the following scientific or technical problem? Cite the specific evidence. (Evaluating, Extended Abstract, Extended Thinking)

- Create a metaphor comparing a scientific concept to a dissimilar object. (For example: Create a metaphor comparing the human brain to a computer.) Use what you know about the concept to explain your comparison in writing. (Evaluating, Relational, Extended Thinking)

- What would the hypothesis be for your experiment? (Evaluating, Extended Abstract, Strategic Thinking and Reasoning)

Social Studies

- Explain a social studies concept. (For example: Explain democracy in your own words.) (Understanding, Uni-structural, Basic Skills and Concepts)

- Create a song, rhyme, or rap to demonstrate your understanding of a concept previously taught. (Creating, Extended Abstract, Extended Thinking)

- Defend your answer to a controversial question. (For example: Defend your answer to the question, *Is technology controlling us, or are we controlling it?*) (Evaluating, Relational, Strategic Thinking and Reasoning)

- Propose an alternative solution to a world problem. (For example: Propose an alternative solution to world hunger.) (Creating, Extended Abstract, Extended Thinking)

It is not important to determine which category of the taxonomies is addressed by a specific question or task. It is more important that most questions being asked are above the *Remembering* or *Recall and Reproduction* levels and that the teacher is modeling the thought processes involved so that students have the metacognitive ability to think about their own thinking.

Which Teacher Interactions Promote Thinking?

A teacher should engage in several additional interactions during instruction to promote quality student thought in the classroom. Four of those interactions follow.

Create the Expectation That All Students Are Capable of Answering Any Question

Over fifty years of research support the fact that teachers get what they expect. This research was grounded in Robert Rosenthal and Lenore Jacobson's much-discussed 1968 study, which came to be known as Pygmalion in the Classroom! The results of 345 experiments on expectations were summarized by Rosenthal and Rubin (1978). A large effect size of 0.70 showed a strong correlation between the expectations of the experimenter and the results of the subjects, whether the experiment occurred in a laboratory setting or in real life. Harris and Rosenthal (1985) examined 135 studies regarding the effects of expectations on certain behaviors. Results indicated that a student's input factors (i.e., sex, age, and ethnicity) were the most important mediators, followed by output factors (i.e., teacher questioning and frequency of interactions), followed by classroom climate, and feedback (i.e., teacher praise and criticism). According to the research on expectations, if teachers do not expect students to become involved in a class discussion and give appropriate responses, students are certainly less likely to do so.

Call on Those Who Volunteer and Those Who Do Not

I cannot tell you the number of times I have conducted model lessons, particularly in a high school, when I have called on a nonvolunteer to answer a question and gotten some form of this response: *Why did you call on me? My hand wasn't raised!* I then proceed to tell the student that a hand does not have to be raised for me to call on him or her, since I consider every student an integral part of the class and I expect each student to know the answer. The research on which the TESA (Teacher Expectations and Student Achievement) Program is based relates that teachers tend to call on students for whom they hold high expectations three to four times more often than those for whom they have low expectations. Teachers gave the following reasons for this practice:

- Students are more likely to hear the right answer.
- It affirms the high achiever.
- It saves instructional time.
- It is affirming to me as a teacher.
- I don't want to embarrass the low achiever.

Consider this scenario. If I am a student who is struggling in your class, I probably have little to no confidence in my ability to do well. To know that I am not going to be called upon sends the expectation that my teacher does not think that I know the answer and is not going to waste the class's time calling on me. Therefore, I do not need to respond in class, complete my homework, or even show up, since I will not be missed! This is not a message that teachers want to send. Specific ways of involving all students before, during, and after a lesson will be delineated in chapters 7–9.

Provide Wait Time for Students Both Before a Question Is Asked and After an Answer Is Given

The concept of *wait time*, or what TESA refers to as *latency*, is based on the research of Mary Budd Rowe (1986), a science teacher who discovered the power of pure silence in K–12 science classrooms. She concluded that there were actually two times in which this silence, or wait time, should occur: (1) after the teacher has asked the question, before calling on a specific student to answer; and (2) after the student responds, before the teacher comments on, affirms, or corrects the response.

If the teacher holds low expectations for the student being called upon, the wait time can be as little as nine-tenths of a second. It is not much better for high achievers, at approximately 2.6 seconds. Research suggests that teachers extend that wait time to a minimum of three to five seconds. When this happens, exciting results appear to follow. More students actually respond. The responses of students are longer, and they are able to provide more evidence to support their answers, pose hypotheses, and speculate. Students actually ask more questions and, most important, achievement improves on the more-challenging test items (Walsh & Sattes, 2005). Benefits for teachers who use wait time include: having to ask fewer questions, but those asked are at higher cognitive levels; more thoughtful teacher responses to students' answers; and higher teacher expectations from students who had not previously participated in the discussion.

Cue, Clue, and Probe if the Answer Is Not Given or Is Incomplete

Cues, clues, and probes are prompts that teachers can use when a student looks puzzled or comes out with the age-old phrase, *I don't know!* Cues are natural follow-ups to the three to five seconds of wait time. When a teacher cues, that teacher may bring back to short-term memory a past learning, ask the student to draw from personal experience, provide a visual reminder, reference a related fact or concept, or provide a mnemonic device. Clues, on the other hand, are more overt. The teacher might give the student a beginning sound, or say, *It starts with a* p, point to the correct answer, or review information needed to answer the question. Then the teacher can ask simple follow-up questions that lead to the original answer. Probes are useful for extending or expanding a student's thinking. If the student's response is incorrect, the teacher may probe for the thinking behind the response such as, *How did you get that answer?*

Answer to Question 6

How can effective questioning show that students are learning?

Other than teacher talk, questioning consumes more class time than any other instructional practice. However, it is not teachers asking questions that correlates with high academic performance; it is the level of questioning that makes the difference. Recitation questions are sometimes needed but often demand lower-level responses. When formulating discussion questions, teachers would do well to create questions or assign tasks of all students that begin with verbs indicative of the higher levels of Bloom's taxonomy, the SOLO taxonomy, or the Depth of Knowledge. If teachers truly believe that all students are capable of responding to those questions, they should engage in the following behaviors: (1) develop and pose relevant, meaningful, quality questions that encourage student thought; (2) select opportunities for students to respond that engage everyone in thinking about the answers; and (3) provide wait time and cues, clues, or prompts, when necessary, so that student answers become more complete and misunderstandings are addressed.

How Do I Know What Students Already Know Before the Lesson?

Oftentimes, when students do well on their formative assessments at the end of a lesson, teachers are pleased at how effectively they taught the lesson. Could it be that many, if not all, students already knew the information before the lesson was even taught? Did the lesson even need to be taught? It is so easy to believe that our excellent teaching made all the difference! Yet, unless there is some way to ascertain what students know before the lesson begins, there is no way to know who should get the credit for the results.

Preassessment activities accomplish a variety of purposes.

- They clarify for the teacher the prior knowledge and skills related to the unit of study.

- The results can guide the planning of the subsequent lessons that will be taught and determine the time that needs to be spent.

- They guide the formation of flexible groups based on the gap between the student's current and desired levels of achievement.

- They give teachers some indication about student interest, values, beliefs, and feelings about the topic.

Pretests are traditional, selected-response ways to ascertain what students already know prior to instruction and are often used just for that purpose. Let's examine some constructed-response alternatives—products and performances—that could provide useful information as well.

Expect Greatness

If teacher expectations appear to have some effect on student performance (Harris & Rosenthal, 1985), all teachers should be expecting the best of students, regardless of the grade level or content area. Visualize each of your students being successful from the first day of the term. Let students know that the school year will be a great one and that you are expecting exceptional performance from them, not only on tests but also during daily work! A student's confidence in his or her ability begins with whether that student believes that the teacher thinks the student capable. In my workshops, I relate the true story of what one teacher did to open the first day of school. She had a piece of paper in her hand. She looked out at her class and down at the paper. Then again, out at the class and down at her paper. Then she commented, "This is going to be such a great year! They gave me every single student I asked for!" The paper she was holding actually had nothing written on it, but wouldn't it be wonderful if each student actually thought that a teacher had personally asked for him or her to be a part of the class?

What's Your Interest?

Positive student-teacher relationships are one of the major correlates to above-average effects on student achievement (Hattie, 2009). If students like you, it is amazing how much more effort they make toward any assessment that you consider important! Those relationships are facilitated when teachers know about the specific likes and dislikes of students. When greeting students at the door or when teaching a lesson, teachers can incorporate those personal interests into the conversation. Administering an interest inventory during the first few days of the school year or semester can garner teachers this information. An inventory should probably include questions such as the following.

- When you have free time, what do you enjoy doing?
- What are your major likes and dislikes?
- What are the names of three of your best friends?
- What are the names of three of your favorite movies?

- What are three of your favorite foods?

- What would you consider to be your talents? In other words, what things are you really good at doing?

- If you could change one thing about you, what would it be?

- What are your favorite subjects in school?

- What do you consider to be important characteristics of a teacher that you like?

- When you are learning, in which activities do you like to engage?

Ways of Knowing

The theory of multiple intelligences was discussed in chapter 2 as one of the theories under consideration when teaching and assessing students. By the way, these *ways of knowing* will be reflected in the activities contained in the next three chapters of this book and are the reasons that the activities will address the learning preferences of all students who reside in your classroom. While identifying each student's intelligence may not correlate to improved academic achievement, it would behoove a teacher to have some idea of students' individual strengths so that those can be incorporated during instruction and cooperative group work. Administering an inventory of multiple intelligences or other comparable learning styles inventory would provide that crucial information. One sample inventory can be found at www.literacyworks.org/mi/assessment/findyourstrengths.html. An individual who takes this inventory, titled Assessment: Find Your Strengths, responds to fifty-six statements regarding his or her multiple intelligences by marking a scale from 1 (*Statement does not describe you at all*) to 5 (*Statement describes you exactly*). My daughter Jessica was administered this same inventory when she applied for the head chef position at a Ritz-Carlton Hotel. Although the inventory is used in the business world for assessing the intelligences of adults, it is also appropriate for middle and high school students. Following are some sample items from the assessment (Multiple Intelligences for Adult Literacy and Education, n.d.).

- Music is very important to me in daily life. (musical)

- I consider myself an athlete. (bodily-kinesthetic)

- I enjoy learning new words and do so easily. (linguistic)

- I do not get lost easily and can orient myself with either maps or landmarks. (spatial)

- I often see mathematical ratios in the world around me. (logical-mathematical)

- I believe I am responsible for my actions and who I am. (intrapersonal)

- I like learning about nature. (naturalist)

- I enjoy new and unique social situations. (interpersonal)

Listen to the Music

Collect music that would be appropriate to use with students in your classroom. So much of today's music would be inappropriate! Any song that includes profanity or sends negative messages should be avoided. As students enter your classroom daily, play either calming or high-energy music depending upon what state or mood you would like to create in their brains. Calming music, at approximately 50–70 beats per minute (which lines up with the heart), puts students' brains in a relaxed state, receptive to learning. High-energy music, at approximately 110–160 beats per minute, motivates and energizes students and may help them attend better to the subsequent lesson. In either case, if students' brains are in a better state for learning, content is more likely to be remembered for the subsequent tests.

It is recommended that you not play music at all when delivering instruction since the brain can pay conscious attention only to one thing at a time and should not have to choose between listening to you and humming along with a favorite tune. Since the conditions for teaching and testing should be the same to facilitate episodic memory, this is another reason why music should not be played during instruction, since it will not be played during testing. Playing music at other times, however—such as during transitions, while working in cooperative groups, or when solving math problems—may put students' brains in such a positive state that memory is facilitated during testing.

A Picture Is Worth a Thousand Words

Put visuals on the walls of your classroom that will facilitate memory during testing, such as the eight parts of speech in language arts, the periodic table in science, or a chronological timeline in history. When students are not looking directly at these visuals, the visuals are still within their peripheral vision and can facilitate memory. Even if these visuals have to be removed prior to testing, if they have been on the wall long enough, students can still visualize them during the test. Remember that the eyes can take in thirty million bits of information per second and process them sixty thousand times faster than words (Jensen, 2007; Gregory & Chapman, 2013).

Entrance Slips

As students enter class on the day that a new unit of study is taught, author and educator Laura Greenstein (2010) gives each student an entrance slip. On that slip, students write their response to a thought-provoking question the teacher poses related to the upcoming unit. These slips can provide diagnostic information to the teacher or pique the interest of students for the unit that they are about to study. Greenstein returns these slips to students at the conclusion of the unit so that they can self-assess whether they would actually change the answer from the initial one or determine how much additional information they have gained during the unit.

K-W-L Chart

A K-W-L graphic organizer covers all the bases. It is one of the most preferred ways to figure out what students already know before the lesson as well as what they want to know about the lesson and, following the lesson, what they have learned. Figure 7.1 provides a visual.

The K-W-L Strategy		
Topic:		
What I Know	What I Want to Know	What I Learned

Figure 7.1: A K-W-L graphic organizer.

Visit www.learningsciences.com/bookresources for a reproducible version of this figure.

Prior to instruction, ask students to brainstorm all the information that they *Know* is related to the topic or concept to be taught. As they share their answers, list them on the organizer. Have students participate in a whole-class discussion either confirming or refuting what they already know. Prior to instruction, have students complete the next column by brainstorming what they *Want* to know regarding the unit of study. Students will keep those ideas in mind as the unit is taught and tested. Following instruction, the last column, what we *Learned*, will be discussed.

Adaptation: If you would like to assess what students already know individually prior to a lesson, have each student complete column one of the graphic organizer on his or her own. As the lesson proceeds, ask students to complete the next two columns individually.

Writing on the Wall

Put poster paper on one wall of the classroom. Give each team a marker and a spot on the poster paper. Prior to your teaching the unit, allow students three minutes to write all that they know about a given topic. These sheets can be saved and the knowledge added to as the unit progresses.

Alphabet Book

Before a unit of study, ask students to brainstorm as many content-area vocabulary words as they can recall that begin with each letter of the alphabet. Put some high-energy music and movement into this activity by giving each student a copy of figure 7.2 (page 83), the Alphabet Book. Have students move around the room and locate other students who can provide content-specific words according to the game directions on the page (Tate, 2014).

This activity can be completed again at the end of the unit to assess how much additional vocabulary students have acquired during the unit.

Three-Corner Preassessment

Use a three-corner preassessment to assess a student's prior knowledge regarding a concept to be taught. Post signs similar to the following in three specific areas of the room.

Rules of the Game: Must have sixty or more words. Can provide twenty words yourself. Must get remaining words from at least eight people outside your family, whose initials will appear on the eight lines below. Must complete game within eight minutes.		A	B
C	D	E	F
G	H	I	J
K	L	M	N
O	P	Q	R
S	T	U	V
W	X	Y	Z

_____ _____ _____ _____ _____ _____ _____ _____

Figure 7.2: Alphabet book.

Visit www.learningsciences.com/bookresources for a reproducible version of this figure.

I know little or nothing about the topic.

I know something about the topic.

I know a great deal about the topic.

Ask students to go to the sign indicative of their level of knowledge on the topic to be taught. This will give the teacher some indication of the level of teaching the lesson requires and the amount of time needed to teach it. The tasks or questions on each sign could be changed according to what the teacher wants to find out prior to instruction (Gregory & Chapman, 2013).

I Know / I Don't Know

When introducing a new topic to students, ask students to raise their hands according to how little or how much they already know about the topic. Have all of those students who know a lot about the topic stand and move to one side of the room. Ask those who know only a little or nothing at all to move to the other side of the room. When you say go, have one student who knows a lot pair with one who does not and take two or three minutes to explain everything he or she knows to his or her partner. If you have more students who do not know than those who do, place them in larger groups with one student who knows in each group. If you do not have any students who know anything, then this activity can be postponed until later in the unit.

SQ3R Technique

When reading informational text (which, by the way, will comprise 70 percent of everything students will read following graduation from high school), ask students to use the following five steps in the SQ3R technique (Tate, 2014).

1. **Survey:** Prior to reading a chapter in a content-area textbook, ask students to preview the chapter. Students should examine headings in bold, captions, illustrations, bold-faced or italicized vocabulary words, and so on.

2. **Question:** Have students turn the bold headings into questions and create additional questions they would like to have answered based on their survey of the material.

3. **Read:** Students should then read to answer the student-generated questions. Answers should be written in the student's own words and not taken verbatim from the text.

4. **Recite:** One student should read each question, and ask another student to tell the answer in his or her own words.

5. **Review:** Answers should be reviewed after a twenty-four-hour period and then from time to time so that memory is facilitated. Remember, *neurons that fire together, wire together*.

Answer to Question 7

How do I know what students already know before the lesson?

Figuring out how much students already know before a lesson is taught can guide a teacher's next steps, such as determining how much time he or she needs to devote to teaching the unit. Written selected-response pretests have always been used to ascertain this information. The constructed-response activities contained in this chapter give teachers other, more engaging options for determining what students already know.

How Do I Know What Students Are Learning During the Lesson?

Classrooms where teachers do all the talking and do not allow for student engagement are classrooms where teachers have little idea what students are really learning. It is absolutely essential that teachers have ways to determine whether students understand and remember the concepts being taught while the lesson is in progress. Assessing during instruction enables teachers to customize teaching to match the existing status of learning (Greenstein, 2010). This data informs practice and allows the teacher to know which of the following steps need to be taken next.

- Review or reteach the entire class.

- Form a flexible group consisting of those few students who need reteaching, while the remainder of the class moves on.

- Ask one student to reteach his or her partner, who simply did not get it.

- Move the entire class on to the next major concept since everybody has it.

A traditional, selected-response test can be given at any point during the lesson. In fact, in school systems across the nation, these tests are called *benchmarks* and are given to ascertain how much students have learned as the teacher moves toward summative assessment. However, there are less formal, but very effective ways to determine the same thing. How much have students learned up to this point in the lesson? Let's look at some constructed ways—products and performances—to accomplish this purpose.

K-W-L Chart (Revisited)

Revisit the second column of the K-W-L chart (see figure 8.1) to recall what students wanted to know about the unit of study. Determine whether those wants are being satisfied by reading some of their original wants aloud and having students address those wants.

The K-W-L Strategy		
Topic:		
What I Know	What I Want to Know	What I Learned

Figure 8.1: A K-W-L graphic organizer revisited.

Sponge It Up

As students enter the classroom daily, have a thought-provoking discussion question or statement related to the unit of study posted in the same place on the document camera or dry-erase board. While students are assembling, they are asked to respond in writing or converse with a partner and respond orally to the posted item. This response may form the basis of the day's discussion. This is an example of a *sponge activity* since it sops up what would otherwise be wasted class time. This activity can also provide insight into students' feelings, values, and beliefs related to the topic of instruction.

Levels of Questioning

Questioning is such an important way to know that students are learning that chapter 6 is devoted entirely to this assessment technique. Be sure to ask both recitation and discussion questions of all students. Chapter 6 delineates the most appropriate times to use either. It also provides verbs that will assist you in formulating questions and assigning tasks that are at the highest levels of cognitive thought.

Choral Responses

When asking specific recitation questions, it may be appropriate for the entire class to respond as a chorus. As students respond orally, you can assess how many students respond appropriately or whether some students do not respond at all. Students can also stand and chorally read short passages of text. For example, when teaching the play *Antigone*, I asked the entire class to stand and read the parts of the Choragus aloud.

Opportunities to Respond

Here are some things to keep in mind when asking questions during the lesson: Always ask the question of the entire class before calling on one student to respond. This is known as *beaming the question*. If you ask the question of one student by name, then all of the other students are *off the hook*. By *beaming the question*, every student has the expectation that he or she could be called on to answer any question.

Volunteers Versus Nonvolunteers

When calling on students, call on both those who raise their hands to answer the question and those who do not. When I conduct a model lesson, I do not know the students nor do they know me. I often ask students to write their first name on an index card, and I then place all cards in a bag. When I need to ask a question, I will reach into the bag and pull out a student's name. This becomes the student to whom the question is directed. Other response opportunities include the following.

- Put Popsicle sticks with students' names in a can. As a question is asked, select a stick; the student whose name appears is chosen to answer the question.

- One teacher whom I observed turned her seventh-grade classroom into a BINGO board. She arranged her students' desks into five straight rows with six chairs in each row. But instead of students sitting in rows *B, I, N, G,* and *O,* they were seated in rows *L, E, A, R,* and *N.* Each desk was numbered 1–6. At the front of the room was a canister with colored chips. As the teacher taught the lesson, she reached into the canister and pulled out chips (e.g., *L3*). If the student was in row *L*, seat three, the next question belonged to him or her. Each student was motivated to pay attention. Once the question was answered, the chip went back into the canister with the understanding that it could be pulled out again at any time.

- Some computer programs randomly select students to respond during the lesson. One such program is called Transum. Students' names are placed into the computer and flashed on the screen randomly when needed.

Wait for Me!

There is research (Rowe, 1986) to support that teachers allow an average of one to three seconds for a student to respond once a question is asked. The Phi Delta Kappa, time-tested program called *TESA* recommends a minimum of five seconds from the time a question is asked until the time the teacher terminates the response opportunity by calling on another student or providing the answer. Why is this wait time necessary? For the extroverted students who are used to shouting out the answers, this wait time gives them a reason to stay silent, while providing time for the introverted students who need to reflect. Tileston (2011) relates that wait time can provide English language learners, who may be reluctant to speak in class due to their unfamiliarity with the language, time to think and gain confidence in their ability. In other words, these precious seconds give every student in class time to think, which improves the quality of each student's response.

Wait Some More!

A second instance during which wait time is needed is after a student has responded. This is especially true when a teacher is asking thought-provoking, open-ended discussion questions. During these times, students do not necessarily have to be called on to respond, and teachers should not affirm or correct student answers. One student's answer may automatically trigger another student's response if time is allotted to silence in between.

Help Is on the Way

If, after five seconds, there is no response from the student or the response is incorrect or incomplete, don't let the student off the hook. It is not acceptable for a student to think that the response *I don't know!* is going to end the discourse. Provide the student with additional information, give him or her a cue or a clue, or rephrase the question. In other words, move the student in the direction of the appropriate answer. The message you send to the students is that you expect them to succeed and will help to accomplish that end.

How Do You Know That?

Oftentimes it is necessary to probe to assess or expand a student's thinking. When you probe, you might be asking follow-up questions to the original one, such as, *How did you get that answer?* or *What caused you to believe that?* One of the most meaningful questions you can ask after a student has responded is, *How do you know that?* Not, *Why did you say that?* The word *why* can often put students on the defensive, but when you ask how they know something, you are asking students to be metacognitive or to think about their thinking. For example, I was teaching a kindergarten lesson when I asked this question: *Where does ham come from?* One student responded, *Ham comes from the turkey*. An initial teacher reaction might be to say, *That is not correct!* Instead, I asked, *How do you know that?* He replied, *Because my mom buys turkey ham!* Now I know what connection he is making in his brain, based on his personal experiences.

Show Me

Give every student a piece of paper or a large index card. On one side of the card, ask the students to write the word *Yes!* and on the other side *No!* When a question is asked to which a yes or no answer is needed, have students turn to the side of the paper that represents their answer. Then on the count of three, ask every student to hold up his or her individual piece of paper simultaneously. Students are told to keep the paper close to their chests so that the teacher can see it but other students cannot. Scan the room, and you will have an informal assessment of how many students are holding up the correct answer.

Adaptation: Rather than *Yes!* or *No!*, students can hold up two-sided papers or cards that say *Agree/Disagree*, *Add/Subtract*, *Multiply/Divide*, or you can have students divide the paper into fourths, with the letters *A*, *B*, *C*, or *D* on each. The students then hold up the correct answer to a multiple-choice question.

Write It Down

Give each student a miniature dry-erase board and a marker, and have them bring in an old sock. (Teachers tell me that the boards can be cut to specifications at Lowe's or Home Depot.) Stop periodically several times during any lesson and ask students to write a short response on the board to a question you have asked. For example, in a science class, students could write the stages of mitosis. When you signal, have every student hold up his or her board simultaneously. This will give you a visual assessment on how many students have written the correct answer and whether any reteaching is necessary.

Quick Writes

Stop periodically during instruction and have students take only a minute to write a brief answer to a question regarding pertinent content. Quick writes are brain compatible since the things that we write down are more likely to be remembered. By the way, the things we write in longhand appear to be remembered longer than the things we type on a computer.

Responding Electronically

With technological advances, students can now respond privately during instruction. Thanks to remotes and clickers, teachers can poll students and collect data instantly from the poll. This data can be continuously collected during the formative assessment process and used to provide feedback to you and to students.

Partner With Me

Assign each student a *close partner*. *Close partners* should sit so close to a student that the student does not have to get up to talk with this person. When content needs to be retaught or an answer discussed, give students opportunities to converse. While those discussions are taking place, observe and take note of those students who are reteaching correctly as well as the quality of the discussions that are occurring (Tate, 2016).

Finger Feedback

When a concept is taught during instruction, students' levels of understanding can be assessed by asking them to raise the number of fingers according to the following scale:

> 5 fingers—completely understand
>
> 4 fingers—understand most of it
>
> 3 fingers—understand half of it
>
> 2 fingers—understand some of it
>
> 1 finger—don't understand any of it

Adaptation: Assess students' level of understanding by having students use their thumbs instead of fingers. Have them do a *thumbs-up* during a lesson if they completely understand, a *thumbs-to-the-side* if they are not sure, and a *thumbs-down* if they simply do not understand.

Help Me, Please!

When you have assigned students seatwork to complete, such as solving math problems independently or writing a composition, you want to be available to provide assistance to those who need it. The problem comes when you may get stuck with one or two students who are struggling and are unable to assess what the remainder of the class is doing. There is a technique called Praise, Prompt, and Leave, developed by an educator named Fred Jones. When practicing this technique, simply look over the shoulder of a student who is working individually, find something that he or she is doing correctly, and praise it. Remember, it is more effective to praise effort than ability. Second, if the student needs help, give a prompt that will move him or her in a more appropriate direction. Last, leave this student and go to another one. In this way, you will be able to see the work of more students. If the prompt doesn't help, find a student who appears to know what he or she is doing and have that student reteach the student who needs help. If you discover through this process that most students are confused, stop the entire class, go to the front of the room, and reteach the concept to the entire class. Repetition is good for all brains (Thomas, 2014).

Sticky Stuff

Give each student a set of small Post-it notes. As the textbook is read and teacher- or student-generated questions are asked, all students are required to find text evidence to support the answer to the question. All students locate the text evidence and mark it by placing a Post-it note in the book.

Adaptation: Students can also use Post-it notes to indicate part of a textbook chapter or story that they do not understand or find confusing. At a given time, students can come back to those sections and discuss them with the teacher or a partner for clarification.

It's All About the Hands

The relationship between the hands and brain activity is so complicated that no one theory can explain it (Jensen, 2001). However, that relationship should be capitalized upon when assessing student learning. Provide students with manipulatives and, while you observe, have them demonstrate their understanding of a concept being taught. For example, in a math class, have students solve a problem using base ten blocks or show a geometric pattern with a geoboard. In a science class, have students conduct an experiment to prove or disprove a hypothesis. Your observations go a long way toward assessing students' understanding while using manipulatives.

Draw It

Good readers reading a story or novel without pictures can visualize the action in the story to comprehend what they are reading. Some students have a difficult time visualizing, since many of the toys that students play with today are accompanied with visuals, which are in living color, no less! Ask students to take out a piece of paper and fold it into fourths. While reading a story aloud to the class, stop and ask students to picture in their minds' eyes what you are reading. Ask them to draw what they are visualizing in one of the squares on the paper. Repeat the procedure three times. Walk around the room and peruse their drawings. From their pictures, you will be able to judge their level of comprehension for story detail.

Move It! Move It!

Finding kinesthetic ways to enable students to respond accomplishes several purposes. First, it facilitates memory. According to David Sousa (2011), when students sit for more than twenty minutes, blood pools in their seats and feet. When they get up and move, that blood is recirculated, and 15 percent of the recirculated blood goes to the brain within a minute, facilitating the growth of dendrites, or brain cells. Second, it is simply more motivating due to the dopamine, a feel-good chemical that is produced when students are in motion. Therefore, when you need students to respond, rather than having them simply raise their hands, have them stand up, wave their hands, pump their fists, or turn around if they agree with an answer and remain seated if they disagree.

Graphic Organizers

One of the best strategies for comprehending a lecture or informational cross-curricular text is a graphic organizer. Graphic organizers are often referred to as thinking maps, mind maps, concept maps, semantic maps, and word webs. They meet the learning needs of both left and right hemispheres of the brain since they are visual representations of linear ideas. The right hemisphere can see the picture while the left hemisphere is reading the words. As you present information during a lesson, create a mind map on a document camera or dry-erase board. Have students copy the graphic organizer in their notes. When you have finished, remove the visual of the organizer you drew and have students turn their copies facedown. Ask the entire class questions regarding what they drew and have them respond chorally. You would be surprised how much students remember when they have a chance to see the visual that accompanies the lecture, to draw the organizer itself, and to visualize what they saw and drew. A visual of a sample mind map is shown in figure 8.2 (page 96).

For samples of additional specific graphic organizers that facilitate comprehension skills, consult the text *Reading and Language Arts Worksheets Don't Grow Dendrites: 20 Literacy Strategies That Engage the Brain*, 3rd ed. (Tate, 2014).

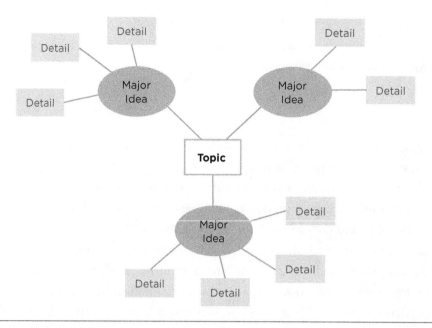

Figure 8.2: Mind map.

Socratic Seminars

Engage students in a Socratic Seminar with the following procedure (Tanner & Cassados, 1998).

1. Determine the main idea of a story, poem, or book that students have already read.

2. Develop a series of discussion questions that encourage students to think at higher levels. Refer to chapter 6 for verbs that facilitate higher levels of thought.

3. Place students in two circles, one inside the other. In the inner circle, seat students who will be a part of the discussion; in the outer circle, seat students who will be taking notes.

4. Initiate a ten- to fifteen-minute discussion by asking a core question in a series of questions to get the dialogue started. Continue to engage students by asking additional questions. To facilitate student thought, remember to provide wait time both before and after you ask the questions.

5. Have a student in the inner or outer circle summarize the major points made during the discussion.

6. Assess students' levels of understanding as you pay attention to who participates and listen to the quality of their responses.

7. Debrief with students by asking for ways in which the seminar could have been improved. Implement any meaningful recommendations during the next seminar.

Read It Closely

Use the following process called *close reading* to enable students to understand complex texts (McLaughlin & Overturf, 2013). The steps can be used with the entire class and may take several days to complete.

1. After little or no prereading discussion, introduce students to the text.

2. *First Reading*—Ask students to read the entire text without help.

3. *Second Reading*—Provide a model of good reading by fluently reading the entire text aloud. Stop periodically to discuss vocabulary, complicated sentence structure, or the social or historical context of the passage. Do not explain the characters, ideas, or specific events in the text. Ask students to discuss the text.

4. Form discussion questions that students can answer only from reading the text, and pose them to the class.

5. *Third Reading*—Have students read the text to locate evidence to answer the text-dependent questions.

6. When necessary, have students use other brain-compatible strategies such as art, music, or graphic organizers to facilitate their comprehension of the text.

7. Have students answer each text-dependent question in one sentence.

8. Assess students' understanding by having them orally or in writing provide an analysis of the text, including text-based evidence in support of their analysis.

Solve It!

Post chart paper all around the walls in mathematics class. Once you have taught a problem-solving strategy, have students work in pairs or trios and proceed to a piece of chart paper. Place a math problem on the document camera or dry-erase board for students to write on the chart paper and solve with their partners. As students work, walk around the room providing individual help to those students who require it and assessing which students have understood the problem-solving strategy you just taught. Give students another problem and repeat the procedure.

Project-Based Learning

Projects are in-depth studies and can capitalize on the interests, learning styles, and curiosity of students, which a selected-response, traditional test never could. These projects are usually grounded in a specific subject area around a specific topic of study. They can be (1) structured with expectations and guidelines spelled out; (2) structured as topic-related, where the student selects a topic of interest and produces a product that shows what has been learned; or (3) structured as open ended, or loosely structured, so that students can draw on their knowledge and creativity. Projects usually begin during the formative assessment stage and may conclude during the summative stage.

Assist students in following these procedures for project work (Gregory & Chapman, 2013).

1. Select a topic.

2. Develop a plan of action including a timeline or cooperative group responsibilities.

3. Implement the plan, which includes gathering ideas, listing resources, determining the format, determining a rubric, conferencing, compiling ideas, and preparing the presentation.

4. Exhibit and present the project.

What Did I Learn?

Tell students that before they leave class daily, they must turn to their close partner and relate one thing that they have learned in class. I call this *job protection* because the first thing that many parents ask when their children get home from school is, *What did you learn in school today?* Most students typically say, *Nothing!* What students tell their partner during this activity is probably the same thing they will tell their parents. It really makes you look like such a great teacher!

Answer to Question 8

How do I know what students are learning during the lesson?

Formative assessments occur during the lesson to inform practice as well as a teacher's next steps for moving students toward proficiency. Benchmark selected-response tests have been used for this purpose. The constructed-response activities contained in this chapter provide teachers with a plethora of engaging ways for teachers to know that students are learning while the lesson is progressing. In this way, teachers will surmise what instructional practices must happen next to help ensure that students will be prepared for summative assessment.

QUESTION 9

How Do I Know What Students Have Learned After the Lesson?

By the time a teacher is ready to give a summative assessment to ascertain what students have learned at the end of a period of study, the results should be of no surprise. If formative assessments are done correctly, there should be a great deal of evidence to support the fact that students have learned what they should have mastered.

Traditional selected-response tests are one way to ascertain this information. In chapter 5, information was provided about how to write questions that truly show what students have learned. However, let's look at constructed-response examples—products and performances—since these, too, can give us valuable information regarding student proficiency throughout and at the end of a unit of study.

K-W-L Chart (Revisited Again)

Students are now ready for the third column in the K-W-L chart (see figure 9.1, page 102). It is time to determine *what students have learned*. You might want to have a brainstorming session in which students call out what they have learned during the unit of study and write down their answers since it makes for a good review. To the class list, add any other pertinent information that you feel is important for the summative assessment. Remember to go back to the original question and make sure students now *know what you expect them to know, understand, or be able to do* as it relates to the unit of study.

The K-W-L Strategy		
Topic:		
What I Know	What I Want to Know	What I Learned

Figure 9.1: A K-W-L graphic organizer revisited again.

Boggle

Boggle is a game that can show you what students remember. Have students take two minutes to review any notes and bring back to short-term memory anything they can recall regarding a concept, novel, or unit of study previously taught. Then have students put the notes away, and give each student two minutes to write down everything they can recall. Each student selects a partner and compares his or her list to the list of the partner. Each student receives one point for every item written down that his or her partner did not list. If an item occurs on both lists, it cancels out. The student in each partnership who earns the most points is the winner.

Adaptation: Rather than looking for differences, have students add the items on their lists to those on the lists of their partners and receive credit for a combined score. The partnership with the largest combined score wins.

Carousel

Place four pieces of chart paper on the wall in four different areas of the classroom. On each piece, write a topic that was taught during the lesson. For example, if a teacher in a social studies class has taught a lesson on the Vietnam War, the four topics could be as follows: *Causes of the War, Countries That Fought in the War, Major Battles and Their Outcomes,* and *Objections to the War.*

Place students in groups of five or six. Give one student in each group a marker and appoint him or her as the scribe. Have one group begin at each piece of chart paper and list everything the group can recall about that topic in two minutes. After two minutes, call "time," and have groups rotate clockwise to the next chart and add to what the initial groups wrote. The process is repeated two additional times until each group has been to every poster. Playing high-energy, toe-tapping music, like Katy Perry's "Roar" or "Happy" by Pharrell Williams, while the groups write and rotate makes this a favorite activity of many students.

Draw It!

When students come in, have bulletin board paper on one wall. Give each student a marker and ask him or her to draw one major concept each student remembers about the unit just taught. Tell them to be prepared to discuss with the class what they drew and how it relates to the unit. When the class is finished, you should have a mural, which can serve as a much-needed review prior to a test. Remember: before it is formally assessed, the brain needs something taught and reviewed at least twice.

Acrostic Topic Activity

When students need to recall important information regarding a unit of study previously taught, ask them to complete the following Acrostic Topic activity. Divide the class into groups of four to six. Provide each group with a large piece of chart paper, with a major topic from the unit written vertically down the left-hand side. This topic will serve as an acronym that each group will use to list facts related to the topic. For example, the following can be used in a social studies classroom:

C   Came to America for religious freedom

O   On long trips in boats

L   Loyalists agreed with the British king.

O   Often people farmed and hunted.

N   No taxation without representation

I   If you wanted independence, you were a patriot.

E   Even kids helped with chores such as cooking or fishing.

S   Some took the Native Americans' land.

Each group shares their finished product with the class. If a group has difficulty coming up with a fact that begins with the designated acronym letter, the group members are free to use their textbooks or the Internet. It is amazing how creative some students can be when given the opportunity (Green & Casale-Giannola, 2011).

Act It Out!

Following a unit of study, have students form cooperative groups of four to six. On an index card, write one important concept from a unit previously studied. You should have as many cards as you have groups. Give each group a card with the task to design a role-play that would demonstrate the concept on the card. Each group should prepare to present the role-play to the class. For example, students could act out the definition of content-area vocabulary words, a scene from a period of history, the steps in a science experiment, or the specific steps in a math word problem. When it is time for the test, it is amazing how much students remember when they can visualize the role-plays that were demonstrated.

Toss Me the Ball

Following a unit of study, have students stand in a circle and participate in a ball toss game. Ask a question of all students, give them three to five seconds to think of an answer, and then toss a Nerf or other soft ball to one student. That student should provide the answer. If the student is unsure, be certain to provide cues, clues, or prompts to assist. If the answer is correct, the student can toss the ball to another student of his or her choice, after you ask the next question and provide wait time. If the answer is incorrect, the ball returns to you (Tate, 2014).

Three-Two-One

At the end of a unit of study, have students respond in writing to the following three prompts:

3—*Three* vocabulary words or key facts from the unit just taught

2—*Two* lingering questions or major ideas from the unit just taught

1—*One* question I still want to ask or way to apply new learning

Have students put their names on their papers so that you can determine how to respond to individual students after this activity. It will also provide feedback as to which vocabulary words, key facts, and major ideas were recalled by the majority of students (Greenstein, 2010).

Jeopardy!

Create a *Jeopardy!* board that reflects the major ideas in a unit just taught. Turn the major ideas into answers for the board. To save time, you may want to have only three columns: $100 (the easiest answers from the unit), $300 (moderately difficult answers), and $500 (the most challenging answers). There should be five answers in each column, which would give you fifteen items on the *Jeopardy!* board. Divide the class into three heterogeneous teams. Each team appoints a facilitator who provides the answer after conferring with the team, and a scribe who keeps track of the points. Teams then compete against one another by taking turns selecting an answer and providing the appropriate question. If the question is correct, the points are added to the score. If the question is incorrect, the points are subtracted. Include two Daily Doubles to make the game more interesting. Play continues according to the rules of the television show until all of the answers have been selected. Any team with money can wager any or all of it during the bonus round. The bonus question should be one of the most challenging. The team with the most money at the end of the game wins. A computerized version of *Jeopardy!* is also available (Tate, 2014).

Frayer Model

The Frayer Model is one type of graphic organizer that teachers can use to help students synthesize information taught and summarize conceptual understanding. Have students write the name of a major concept already taught in the circle in the middle of the model. Then ask students to complete the other four sections by writing a definition of the concept in the top left-hand box, important facts and other characteristics related to the concept in the top right-hand box, examples of the concept in the bottom left-hand box, and nonexamples of the concept in the bottom right-hand box. See figure 9.2 for a blank form.

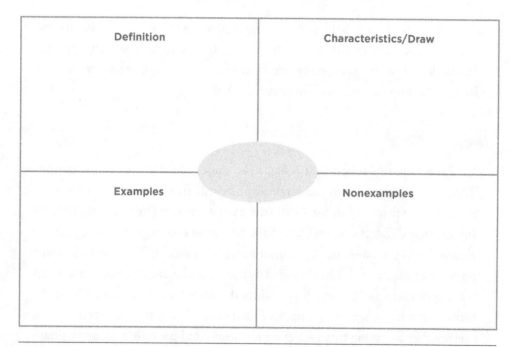

Figure 9.2: The Frayer Model.

Visit www.learningsciences.com/bookresources for a reproducible version of this figure.

What's on the Test?

Following a unit of study, have students form cooperative groups (families) of four to six. Ask each group to write at least five recitation and/or discussion questions that could be on the subsequent test. Ask students to use the criteria for writing quality questions (found in chapter 5 of this book) in order to guide the formation of those questions, and ask them to incorporate the verbs in chapter 6 into the question stems. Students could then exchange questions with another family and answer that family's questions.

Adaptation: This activity can be turned into the competition of a game if, after the questions are written, they are placed on a piece of colored paper and made into a paper airplane. Each family designates one student in the family to fly the plane to a specific destination in the room. The plane that comes closest to the destination without going past is the winner. The person who flew each plane then picks up the plane of another family, takes it back to his or her family, and the questions on the new plane are answered. Teachers can assess the quality of the questions and how well they are answered, while students share orally. Some of the best student questions can be put on the actual test.

More Is Needed

If, after a lesson or unit of study is taught, there are students whose assessment results indicate the need for additional instruction, or if you have students whose knowledge needs to be extended or enriched, specialized learning centers and/or computer programs can be used to meet individual or small-group needs. Flexible groups can also be formed for the purpose of reteaching or enrichment. Be certain that if specific brain-compatible strategies were used during the lesson, different ones may need to be incorporated for remediation or enrichment.

Answer to Question 9

How do I know what students have learned after the lesson?

Once a unit of study is complete, summative assessment ensues. Traditional selected-response tests, such as end-of-course tests, are often the order of the day. However, there are constructed-response tasks in which students can engage to show that they have learned what you need them to know. Many of these types of tasks will prepare students to score higher on their selected-response assessments. The activities contained in this chapter address a variety of the multiple intelligences and learning modalities of students and should be used if you really want to know whether students are learning.

How Can Checklists Be Used to Assess Student Learning?

There is a school of thought that students should be producing their own knowledge rather than reproducing that of their teachers. Some traditional assessments are ways that teachers have of knowing whether students can reproduce or regurgitate what they have learned. Authentic assessments enable students to use their creativity to produce original products and performances. However, teachers tend to shy away from authentic assessment items for a number of legitimate reasons. Haladyna (1997) delineated a few of those reasons:

Cons

- It takes more teacher time to score student responses.
- Even when a scoring guide is included, scoring is less accurate due to multiple interpretations of the responses.
- Scoring guides can include highly subjective wording.
- Students may not be able to communicate effectively in writing what they actually know and understand.

The cons, however, may be outweighed by the pros, particularly for some assessment tasks.

Pros

- Constructed-response tasks are usually more challenging than selected-response questions.

- Students must create an original response rather than selecting one that has been provided.

- These tasks are more indicative of student thought and understanding, which may be incorrectly inferred from selected-response items. (Students can luck up and get the right answer.)

- Constructed-response items provide more information about what instructional steps should happen next.

- The assessment items are usually easier to write than good, high-level, selected-response questions.

- Several concepts and skills for a unit can be measured with just one or two constructed-response questions.

If we *begin with the end in mind* when planning a lesson, as suggested in chapter 4, then the first question must be: *What should students know and be able to do by the time instruction has ended?* To answer that question, teachers may simply need to know whether knowledge has been acquired or a behavior is present. If either of those is the case, a checklist may suffice. The checklist can be both a teacher's most valuable instructional and assessment tool and a student's helpful organizational and study skills tool (Burke, 2010). It is an assessment strategy that can be used during the formative or summative stages to determine if individual students or the entire class has demonstrated the desired skills or behaviors necessary to meet a curricular objective or standard.

Using a checklist during formative assessment is an uncomplicated and expedient way to observe and record those required skills and behaviors that must be demonstrated during the summative evaluation. By the time of the summative assessment, there should be very few, if any, surprises. For example, if the checklists show that the class has mastered the criteria, then, by all means, celebrate and move on! If only a few students have not mastered the skill or behavior, there is time to form a flexible group for those who need it and reteach, while the remainder of the class moves on. If the checklists show that the majority of the class has not mastered the criteria, there should be time to reteach the entire class using a different instructional methodology.

Multistep Checklists for Students

As an organizational and study skills tool, checklists serve as the *scaffolding*, or support, students need as they undertake a task, since checklists have the ability to divide a difficult, multistep task into manageable steps.

Listed below is a personal example to illustrate the value of an organizational checklist. When I was working on my doctorate in educational leadership, I divided a major, multistep, complex task into smaller steps, which I found manageable. My checklist consisted of the following.

- ☐ Complete coursework (I listed each course separately).
- ☐ Celebrate!
- ☐ Pass comprehensive exams.
- ☐ Celebrate!
- ☐ Decide on dissertation topic.
- ☐ Select members of committee.
- ☐ Research selected topic.
- ☐ Defend proposal.
- ☐ Celebrate!
- ☐ Collect and analyze data.
- ☐ Write remaining chapters of dissertation (I listed each chapter separately).
- ☐ Conduct final defense.
- ☐ Celebrate!

I kept telling myself that if I completed this checklist, one step at a time, I would wake up one morning with my doctorate in hand. And I did! Other students who started out with me did not finish. I often wonder whether they, too, had checklists that divided this arduous task into manageable steps.

Notice that I did not wait until the end of the entire process to celebrate. I visualized myself completing each major step on the checklist successfully. After each major success, I celebrated! Since success breeds success, and success instills confidence, then students should do the same thing. If I taught a student who received a 65 percent on his last test and a 73 percent on the next test, there is cause for celebration. Is the student passing? No! Is the student moving in the right direction? Yes! The celebrations enable the brain to visualize achieving an even higher score on the next assessment.

Let's consider a K–12 academic example in which an arduous task was divided into multiple components. When Jessica was in fifth grade, her social studies teacher incorporated a project as a summative assessment activity, rather than a traditional, selected-response test, at the conclusion of their unit on the Civil War. The project was the production of a Civil War newspaper. Jessica and her parents were given a checklist of the things that her newspaper had to include. The list was as follows.

- ☐ A title
- ☐ A cost
- ☐ A slogan
- ☐ An index
- ☐ A feature story with an accompanying visual
- ☐ A crime story
- ☐ An advertisement
- ☐ Three additional articles, at the discretion of the student, describing Civil War events

Jessica is now in her thirties, and she still remembers this project and so do I. It was so much more memorable than a selected-response test would have been. An additional advantage of this one project was that the teacher integrated the social studies objectives regarding the Civil War with the language arts objectives regarding the parts of a newspaper. How ironic that in this day and age, when many people get their news from the Internet, the latter objectives may no longer be relevant. More than twenty years later, Jessica still remembers how she responded to her assignment.

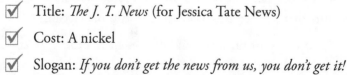

- ☑ Title: *The J. T. News* (for Jessica Tate News)
- ☑ Cost: A nickel
- ☑ Slogan: *If you don't get the news from us, you don't get it!*
- ☑ Index: Featured all parts of the paper with the accompanying page numbers

☑ Feature story: "The Assassination of Abraham Lincoln," with an accompanying picture of Lincoln. (This was before we had access to the Internet and the first time that Jessica realized that you do not cut a picture of Abraham Lincoln out of the encyclopedia.)

☑ Crime story: John Wilkes Booth suspected of being the shooter of Lincoln

☑ Advertisement: Horse shoes sold for $.50

☑ Three additional articles at Jessica's discretion

Jessica appreciated the checklist since it served as a consistent reminder of what her newspaper should include. The checklist enabled us, as her parents, to look at the finished product prior to having Jessica turn it in to her teacher, which would ensure that she had not omitted any required elements that would negatively impact her grade. The teacher used a checklist to assess each student's newspaper and laminated the paper for posterity. Jessica received an A and was so proud of what she had accomplished!

Components of a Checklist for Teachers

Some of the most common components of an individual student's organizational and assessment checklist include the following (Burke, 2010).

☐ Title (name of the task being assessed)

☐ Student's name, class period, date

☐ Standard(s) the checklist addresses

☐ Brief description of the task the student is completing

☐ Performance indicators or major chunks of the task, listed in bold and organized in sequential order

☐ Subpoints or subskills listed under each category, indented or bulleted and typically presented in the form of a question

☐ Scoring columns to the right for rating the subskills, which could range from a simple *Not yet* or *Yes*, to a numerical score

☐   A section for student comments about his or her performance
and a place for teacher feedback with the signatures of both

☐   A scale that shows how the total point values translate into a
letter grade, percentage grade, or a proficiency level

Figure 10.1 (page 115) provides a template that teachers can use to develop a checklist for an individual student.

Figure 10.2 (page 116) provides a template that teachers can use to develop a checklist for an entire classroom of students.

Answer to Question 10

How can checklists be used to assess student learning?

Constructed responses—products and performances—encourage students to use their higher-level cognitive skills of applying, synthesizing, and creating. They should be used throughout a unit to formatively assess students. However, some students may have a difficult time planning their time and effort in order to complete the project. Checklists can be a meaningful tool for dividing a complex task into manageable parts and for keeping students on track during a lengthy task such as a project. Checklists can also assist teachers in ascertaining which skills, concepts, or dispositions students have acquired throughout the unit. Some sample checklists have been included in this chapter. If a more qualitative assessment is needed, rubrics could be more appropriate. Chapter 11 is devoted to the use of rubrics for this purpose.

Title: _____		
Student: _____		
Subject: _____	Period: _____	
Standard/Objective: _____		
Product/Performance: _____		
Indicators	**(-)**	**(+)**
Major Category: _____		
•		
•		
•		
Major Category: _____		
•		
•		
•		
Major Category: _____		
•		
•		
•		
Teacher Comment: _____ _____		
Student Comment: _____ _____		
Teacher Signature: _____ _____		
Student Signature: _____ _____		

Figure 10.1: A product/performance checklist template that teachers can use for an individual student.

Visit www.learningsciences.com/bookresources for a reproducible version of this figure.

Directions: Write the skills to be observed on the top slanted lines.

Teacher: _____ **Class:** _____ **Date:** _____

Targeted Skills: _____

Ratings:

   + = Often Observed

   √ = Seldom Observed

   ○ = Not Observed

STUDENTS' NAMES						COMMENTS
1.						
2.						
3.						
4.						
5.						
6.						
7.						
8.						
9.						
10.						
11.						
12.						
13.						
14.						
15.						
16.						
17.						

Figure 10.2: An observation checklist template that teachers can use for an entire classroom of students.

Visit www.learningsciences.com/bookresources for a reproducible version of this figure.

Sometimes a teacher will want to know whether the entire class has understood a concept or can demonstrate a skill.

QUESTION 11

How Can Rubrics Be Used to Assess Student Learning?

Constructed responses are more difficult to grade. There is no getting around that fact! This is why many teachers avoid products and performances as summative types of assessment. The previous chapter discussed checklists. There are times when a checklist will suffice, such as when delineating the steps in a multistep process, during observations, or when determining the presence or absence of a skill, behavior, disposition, or ability. However, when grading the quality of a product or performance, checklists can be insufficient.

Advantages of Using Rubrics

Rubrics are a necessary part of assessment. A rubric is a scoring guide that teachers can use to evaluate students' constructed responses. Rubrics enable teachers to determine various levels of quality in students' products and performances. Rubrics extend checklists since they describe the different levels of quality that can be achieved on every evaluative criterion (Burke, 2010).

Lowers Students' Stress Levels Regarding Teacher Expectations

When I was in school, I was considered a good student who made As the majority of the time. My attitude toward assessment could be summed up in the following statement: *Guess what the teacher is going to put on the test.* If I guessed right and studied the right content, I made my usual A. If I guessed incorrectly and studied hard, but studied the wrong content, I did not make the grade I desired. This really upset me. I would be so stressed that I could not sleep the night before test day. When I sat down in class, I would peruse the entire test before I began. If my teachers had given me the opportunity to create constructed responses and provided me with the specific criteria on which I would be assessed, my schooling would have been so much less threatening. With a rubric, students understand that the result of their academic success is totally within their control. If they are willing to work for the A, that A can be achieved.

Provides Predictability and Patterning

A positive learning environment needs to be predictable. According to Judy Willis (2006), when the limbic system and the affective filter of the brain are assured of predictability, the brain processes information more efficiently. The circuits of the neurons are attuned for patterns, so when sequences of behavior are predictable, they are brain compatible.

Rubrics are a powerful tool for achieving this patterning and predictability. They provide students with an outline of the criteria to be evaluated in determining the final grade. This knowledge allows students to see the relationship between their work, effort, and attitude, which ultimately leads to their success. Students then become partners with the teacher and are more engaged and confident, because they see a process that is predictable with a clearly defined outcome.

In addition, Willis relates, rubrics help students set specific goals in a number of different areas of achievement, not just in the final product. These areas might include effort, organization, cooperation, proper use of resources, and metacognition. Some of the same qualities are part of the executive function of the frontal lobe of the brain, which is the highest form of true learning.

Serves as a Visualization Stimulus

Earlier in this book, we talked about the power of visualization for the brain. When students are given rubrics at the beginning of a unit of study, they can see themselves experiencing success. Just as athletes visualize themselves scoring the touchdown or hitting the home run, students' visualizations get their brain circuits in line with the muscle movements to accomplish whatever is being imagined. Images of the brain even show that when students begin to think about a certain type of learning, the area of the brain that controls that type of learning becomes activated. Rubrics not only help students see the big picture, they also enable students to see the parts that comprise the big picture as well.

Shows Students What Quality Work Actually Looks Like

According to Wiliam (2011), when students have time to think through and discuss the rubrics for judging their own work that have been shared with them, they are more likely to become aware of the true definition of quality. In fact, I tell teachers that when using a rubric for grading, show students an example of what the highest level of proficiency on the rubric actually looks like. If level five is the highest level, students should see what a level-five essay, poster, PowerPoint, or brochure looks like. If the same product or performance was used the previous year, the best quality examples should be saved and shown to students the following year prior to beginning the project, so that students can view actual examples of excellence.

Helps to Ensure That All Products and Performances Are Judged by Identical Standards

Rubrics assist teachers in making a subjective assignment more objective. For example, in the workshop, I ask teachers to give a numerical grade to an essay written by an eighth grader on the topic of why women should receive pay equal to that of men. We examine the essay on the document camera and then individually assign it a grade. The grades for the entire class usually range from 60 percent to 93 percent. That is a difference on the same assignment between a failing grade and a very good essay. If a rubric had been constructed prior to the writing of the essay, with the criteria and indicators on which the essay would be graded, the grades would have been more objective, consistent, and fair to all students.

Enables Teachers to Provide Specific Feedback to Students Regarding the Quality of Their Work

Chapter 13 will deal with the feedback students receive during peer- and self-assessment. Rubrics are excellent tools for helping students self-assess their own work in an effort to improve their products or performances during the formative assessment process. Students know in advance exactly what criteria will be used in assessing their work. In turn, parents also know what quality work in your class should look like and what criteria are reflected by each grade given. Parent/teacher conferences become much easier when there is definitive evidence for the reason a student received a particular grade.

Types of Rubrics

There are three major types of rubrics—generalized, analytic, and weighted. The characteristics of each type will be described in the following sections.

Generalized

Generalized rubrics focus on complex questions such as, *What constitutes an exceptional science project?* These types of rubrics delineate the critical attributes of a task. They are used more often for final judgments during summative assessment since, during formative assessment, the feedback you get from generalized rubrics is not specific enough for students to improve the quality of their work.

Analytic

When using an analytic rubric, a teacher has to identify specific knowledge and/or skills that a student must demonstrate when completing a specific task. The analytic rubric lists indicators such as thinking strategies, conceptual understandings, application of those understandings, process skills, and so forth (Burke, 2010). It assigns a rating to describe mastery and a separate score for each dimension. These are beneficial during formative instruction since they can provide feedback to students and inform teachers about ways to adjust their instruction.

Weighted

There are times when teachers may consider some criteria on an analytic rubric to be more critical to instruction than other criteria. Teachers might think, therefore, that they deserve more consideration in the scoring. This critical criteria may include the weekly focus of instruction; may relate to an important learning standard, goal, or objective; or may address a key skill that will be assessed on an upcoming standardized test. If this is the case, some criteria on the rubric can be weighted to reflect its level of importance. For example, if the criterion score is a 3, that 3 can be weighted by multiplying it by a 2 or a 3 when determining the final score, depending on that criterion's level of importance.

CRI When Thinking of Rubrics

When considering the use of a rubric to assess students' products and performances, start at the beginning with a good *CRI*. No, I am not asking you to shed tears. *CRI* is a mnemonic device for the three components of a simple analytic scoring rubric.

> **C** stands for the *criteria*, or *dimensions*, of the product or performance to be assessed. In other words, what are the categories to be considered during the assessment process? Most rubrics have between four and eight criteria, or dimensions.

> **R** stands for *rating scale*. In other words, how are the criteria or dimensions going to be assessed? Most rating scales have between three and five levels of performance, with the lowest number typically assigned to the lowest acceptable level of performance and the highest number assigned to the highest level. When constructing a rubric, it is often better to determine what would constitute the lowest and highest level of performances before determining the medial levels, which are more difficult to discern.

> **I** stands for a continuum of *indicators* that will define every level of the dimension. The indicators should be written in student-friendly language and exhibit a clear difference in progression of the levels of performance required.

If you want rubrics to be effective measures of assessment, they should be easily understood. In chapter 3, brain assumption 6 notes that information is more easily learned and remembered when the environment is relevant and authentic. In other words, anytime you are trying to get students to understand a challenging concept, figure out where that concept shows up in the real world. Therefore, to enable teachers to understand how to construct rubrics, we will begin by constructing a real-world rubric, one for planning a birthday party (see figure 11.1, page 122). In this rubric, there are three criteria. They are location/entertainment, food, and gifts. There are four numbers on the rating scale, with 1 being the lowest acceptable level and 4 being the highest. There are twelve missing indicators on the rubric, four for each criterion. Teachers in my classes have fun working with their cooperative groups to fill in the indicators. By the way, in one class I taught, one group of teachers listed a number 1 indicator for the criterion of location and entertainment as a club with ninety-year-old Chippendales dancers. Please don't visualize that! It is not pretty!

Criteria	4	3	2	1
Location/ Entertainment				
Food				
Gifts				

Figure 11.1: A rubric for planning a birthday party.

Let's apply CRI to the rubric as though it were for planning a fiftieth birth-day party. (If I assist students with rubrics, a more relevant, authentic one would be for planning a sixteenth birthday party.) Some completed sample indicators are listed in figure 11.2.

Criteria	4	3	2	1
Location/ Entertainment	Hotel ballroom / dancing with live band	Restaurant chosen by host / live jazz ensemble	Home of a friend / music from iPod	Media center at school / music from iPod
Food	Plated dinner (five-course meal)	Guest selections from restaurant menu	Hot dogs Hamburgers Chips Cake Punch	Cake Punch Nuts Mints
Gifts	All guests contribute to a Hawaiian vacation for honoree	Gifts of guests' choosing	Gag gifts for a fifty-year-old	Cards only

Figure 11.2: A rubric for planning a fiftieth birthday party.

Figures 11.3, 11.4 (page 124), and 11.5 (page 125) show samples of completed rubrics in the areas of science, English, and mathematics, respectively. There is an additional rubric in chapter 13 that can be used as students engage in peer assessment. Refer to figure 11.6 (page 126) for a sample analytic rubric template, which you can use as is or adapt to meet the needs of your students.

Curricular Objective: Compare and contrast the physical attributes of planets.

Product/Performance: Planet poster

	4	3	2	1	SCORE
Criterion 1 Factual Info Regarding Planet	Poster contains three facts (regarding size, position, and orbit time).	Poster contains two facts (regarding size, position, or orbit time).	Poster contains only one fact (regarding size, position, or orbit time).	Facts are omitted or inaccurate.	
Criterion 2 Additional Facts of Interest	Four or more additional interesting facts included.	Three additional interesting facts included.	Two additional interesting facts included.	No facts or only one additional interesting fact included.	
Criterion 3 Illustration of Planet	At least three colors used in drawing; no erasures or cross-outs.	Two colors used in drawing; no erasures or cross-outs.	Only one additional color used; erasures and cross-outs.	Black-and-white drawing only; erasures and cross-outs.	
					TOTAL

Figure 11.3: A sample of a completed science rubric.

Curricular Objective: Write arguments to support claims with clear reasons and relevant evidence.

Product/Performance: Persuasive essay

	4	3	2	1	Score
Criterion 1 Opening	The hook captures the reader's attention immediately.	The hook is present but weak.	The hook does not relate to the essay.	No hook to engage the reader.	
Criterion 2 Position Statement	Position is clearly stated and maintained, and references to the issue are stated.	Position is stated and maintained, but references to the issue are missing.	Position is stated but not throughout the paper.	Thesis statement cannot be determined.	
Criterion 3 Supporting Information	Evidence and examples clearly support the position and are sufficient.	Evidence clearly supports the position but is insufficient.	Evidence to support the position is limited.	The position is not supported by evidence.	
Criterion 4 Closure	The closure clearly restates the position at the beginning of the closing paragraph.	The position is restated in the closing paragraph.	The closing statement does not restate the position.	There is no closing statement.	
Criterion 5 English Grammar and Usage	Essay has no errors in grammar and usage.	Essay has one or two errors in grammar and usage.	Essay has three or four errors in grammar and usage.	Essay has five or more errors in grammar and usage.	
					TOTAL

Figure 11.4: A sample of a completed English rubric.

Curricular Objective: Solve real-life math problems using numerical and algebraic expressions and equations.

Product/Performance: Solve real-life math problems and present to class.

	4	3	2	1	Score
Criterion 1 **Problem Solving**	No errors evidenced when solving problems.	Very few errors evidenced when solving problems.	Numerous errors evidenced when solving problems.	No evidence that the problems are understood.	
Criterion 2 **Use of Math Vocabulary**	Math vocabulary is extensive and correctly used throughout.	Math vocabulary is used correctly.	Some math vocabulary used, but incorrectly.	No math vocabulary used.	
Criterion 3 **Application of Math Skills**	Clear application of math skills.	General application of math skills.	Limited application of math skills.	Little or no application of math skills.	
Criterion 4 **Presentation**	Solution is shown in an easy-to-follow, step-by-step model.	Steps and solution are shown logically.	Solution is difficult to follow at times.	Steps in the solution cannot be followed.	
					TOTAL

Figure 11.5: A sample of a completed mathematics rubric.

Curricular Objective: _____

Product/Performance: _____

	4	3	2	1	Score
Criterion 1					
Criterion 2					
Criterion 3					
Criterion 4					
					TOTAL

Figure 11.6: A sample analytic rubric template.
Visit www.learningsciences.com/bookresources for a reproducible version of this figure.

Be *SAD* When Thinking of Rubrics

When creating relevant rubrics, not only do you want to start with a CRI but you should also be *SAD*. *SAD* is another mnemonic device, which stands for the following three attributes of an effective rubric:

> **S** stands for *standardized*. Systems for scoring rubrics can be inconsistent. Whereas some school districts require teachers to afford a 4 on the rubric to students who meet state standards, other districts require teachers to give a 3 if they meet state standards and

a 4 if they exceed standards (Burke, 2010). The same thing happens when teachers at the same grade level and the same school have different ways of determining scores. When participants complete the birthday party rubric above, nothing is standardized. What is a 1 on the rating scale for one group is a 2 or 3 for another group. A birthday party at Chuck E. Cheese's for a fifty-year-old is probably less than a 1. For my grandchild Christian, it is a 4. In fact, that was exactly where her fifth birthday party was.

When a grade level or a department plans a product or performance to determine whether students are really learning, teachers should work together to be certain that the same rubric is consistently used in every class and applies to all students involved in the project or performance. Teachers should reach consensus as to what each indicator should include and how it should be rated. Many textbooks and curriculum guides contain rubrics that have already been developed to assess major concepts. Teachers may want to use those rubrics rather than develop new ones, which may not be any better than the ones already provided.

A stands for *attainable*. When we plan the birthday party rubric, oftentimes a 4 on the rating scale is actually unattainable. Since I purposely do not give participants a spending limit for the party, teachers list things like an around-the-world cruise with cruise ship entertainment and unlimited buffets as a 4 for location/entertainment and food, and a new car as a gift. We then discuss that the highest level of a rubric needs to be attainable. If you are developing a rubric, students need to perceive themselves as capable of achieving the highest level of that rubric. I recommended earlier in this chapter that students should be shown what the highest level looks like so they will know to what to aspire.

D stands for *defendable*. While a constructed-response assessment could never be as objective as a selected-response assessment, every effort should be made to ensure that the rubric is the least subjective as possible. If a parent comes in and wants to know why her child's poster received a 3, and not a 4, on the rubric, a teacher should be able to definitively respond with the difference between the indicators of a 3 and a 4. In other words, the score given on the rubric should be explained and defended to anyone who asks.

Teachers are busy people, and rubrics, while essential, can be time consuming. But they are worth the effort if we truly want to know whether our more creative students are really learning and whether all students are participating in relevant, authentic projects that call for them to think at higher cognitive levels. Visit www.rubistar4teachers.org for assistance in creating rubrics for your project-based learning activities. Teachers can select customizable rubrics according to the content area being taught or type of assessment desired.

Answer to Question 11

How can rubrics be used to assess student learning?

Constructed responses give students authentic ways to show what they are learning during the formative assessment process. However, they are harder to grade. Rubrics should be used when assessing students' products and performances, since they show what true quality looks like and make grading less subjective. An analytic rubric is the most beneficial type to teachers during the formative assessment stage since they can provide feedback as to what students need to do to improve their products and performances, and teachers have opportunities to adjust their instruction. The three parts of an analytic rubric are the criteria, rating scale, and indicators. Rubrics should also be standardized, attainable, and defendable.

QUESTION 12

How Do We Know What Students Are Learning When They Work Together?

An overemphasis on traditional assessment fosters an atmosphere of stress and competition in the classroom. The message becomes who can outscore whom on teacher-made and standardized tests. While a competitive atmosphere is motivating to some students, particularly the high-achieving ones, many see those assessment results as an indication of their inferiority. I will never forget that in one class I taught, a teacher related this story. His middle school math teacher always passed back the test papers in descending order with the highest scores on the top of the pile and the lowest on the bottom. Since he did not consider himself a good student in math, his test papers were always at or near the bottom of the stack and every other student in his class knew it. He commented that to this very day, he couldn't stand math. Some good came out of this experience, though. Since he is now a teacher, he has vowed never to make the same mistake: to cause his students feelings of inferiority by the order in which he returns test papers. By the way, he did not become a math teacher!

It may be very advantageous, for several reasons, for students to work with one another at specific times during a class period. When they say *two heads are better than one*, they are not kidding! It is amazing how performance is improved even when adults have an opportunity to talk with one another about what they are doing. For example, in one class I teach, I ask participants to write down all they can remember about a lesson just taught regarding the physiology of the brain. They are required to recall at least twelve brain facts to receive a grade of A on the task. Usually 5 to 10 percent of the class achieves this grade when they work individually. Then I have each participant pair with a peer and compare lists. By the time each participant has retaught his or her partner the facts I have taught them, at least 90 percent of the class receives an A.

Yet, when I was taught to teach more than forty years ago, if two students were talking about their content, they were accused of cheating. You were never supposed to discuss what you were learning!

Hopefully in every classroom today, that paradigm has changed. Brain research has informed our practice. If I am given an opportunity to teach what I have learned to someone else, I will retain at least 70 percent of what I say as I talk to him or her and 90 percent of what I talk about as I accomplish a task (Ekwall & Shanker, 1988). According to Hattie (2009), the total effects of students teaching one another in class assists with students regulating themselves and being in control of their own learning. Since *the ability to participate with people from diverse backgrounds and teach others new skills* (SCANS, 1991) is a workplace competency, when teachers enable students to teach one another and participate in cooperative groups in class, they are helping students to become career ready better than any traditional assessment could ever do.

Cooperative learning is more than just seating students in groups and expecting them to work together to get an assigned task accomplished. In fact, the major complaint from many students is that when placed in a group, one or two students end up doing all the work while the others allow this. According to Roger and David Johnson (2002), five structures facilitate *cooperative interdependence* among students, which can turn group work into cooperative learning. Those five structures are discussed in the following sections.

Positive Interdependence

Positive interdependence occurs when students actually believe that the individual effort of each person in the group benefits not only each individual but also the group as a whole. The motto of the group becomes, *we sink or swim together*. The following instructional activities assist teachers in determining whether students in the group are actually participating and learning.

Group Roles

Be certain that students in the group have a role in helping the group to function effectively. While it is not necessary for every student to have a specific role every time a cooperative group is convened, this practice does facilitate student engagement.

In a group of four to six students, you might need only two roles. However, in a group of four, try not to assign three roles, which will leave one student without a role. Listed below are some roles that could be assigned for students to fill (Tate, 2010).

- **Facilitator:** Leads the group discussions or presents the group's findings to the class. Students with high interpersonal intelligence make great group facilitators.

- **Scribe:** Takes notes and writes down anything the group has to submit in writing. Students with intrapersonal intelligence are reflective and may make good note takers.

- **Materials manager:** Collects the necessary materials for the group to accomplish the task and passes them out to the group members. Your bodily-kinesthetic learners who need desperately to get up will appreciate being given this role.

- **Timekeeper:** Keeps the group abreast of the time restraints and informs the group when half the time is over and when only a few minutes are left.

- **Reporter:** Gives an oral report or presentation to the class of the group's findings.

- **Process observer:** Collects data and gives the group feedback on how well they practiced the targeted social skills during the activity. Since a process observer cannot talk while observing, you might want to assign this role to the most talkative student in each group.

Each student can be assessed in terms of how well he or she fulfilled the assigned role. Group roles should be rotated so that no one student ends up filling the same role continually.

I Help You, You Help Me

Students work together in cooperative groups to prepare one another for an upcoming test or to review a concept previously taught. Each student then takes the test individually. If every student in the group exceeds his or her individual score on the previous test, however, each student in the group gets a certain number of points added to his or her score. In this way, students' scores are helped only by their willingness to work with another student in the group prior to the test.

Share the Wealth

Cooperative groups are provided with only one copy of a handout, piece of chart paper, or any other material needed to complete a cooperative learning assignment. The materials manager retrieves the necessary materials and hands them to the facilitator. All students in the group must work together to accomplish the task since there is only one copy of the resource available to the group.

We All Agree!

Students work together in cooperative groups to reach consensus on an assignment, such as math problems given for homework. Each student brings his or her completed homework to the group and confers about the answers to each problem. If answers differ, students discuss why their answer is the correct one. Once consensus is reached, all students put their initials on one paper indicating that they agree with the answers. That paper is submitted to the teacher as the group's best effort, and then all students in the group receive the grade that has been assigned to the one paper. This activity expedites grading for you since, instead of grading each student's paper, you are grading only one paper per group.

Individual Accountability

Individual accountability refers to the fact that although students are working together, each student in the group is equally responsible for demonstrating individual knowledge of the content. In this way, one student cannot take on all of the responsibility for completing the group assignment while the remainder of the group watches it happen. The following activities may help to ensure individual accountability in the classroom.

Each One Teach One

Have students work in pairs. Have one student in each pair reteach a concept just taught to his or her partner. Use observation to ascertain whether the concept is being taught correctly. If too many students are not doing an adequate job of reteaching, stop everyone, go to the front of the class, and teach the concept again. Remember, the brain needs to hear something at least three times before it begins to stick.

Be Prepared

When a cooperative group works together to accomplish a task, build in accountability by telling students that everyone in the group must be prepared since upon completion of the task, any student in the group could be randomly called upon to respond on behalf of the group. This response could include answering a question the group is discussing, orally solving a math problem that the group has been working on, or making some other type of presentation. The group grade could become dependent on the performance of the chosen student.

Jigsaw

One way to help students feel individually accountable is to make them responsible for teaching one part of a lesson to the entire cooperative group. Put students in heterogeneous groups and have them participate in an activity called *jigsaw*. In *jigsaw*, one student in each cooperative group has a piece of the puzzle. Once the puzzle is put together, a whole is created. The procedure for *jigsaw* is as follows (Tate, 2010).

1. Assign one person in each cooperative group the same part of the text. Allow time for students to read and prepare to teach their parts either in class or for homework.

2. Have students confer in class with students in other groups who are teaching the same part for the purpose of comprehending the text and receiving and giving ideas for teaching it to their original groups.

3. Ask students to return to their original cooperative groups. Provide an allotted time, such as two minutes, for all students to take turns teaching their content. If a student finishes before time is called, questions can be asked for clarification or information added. The student who has the next part should not proceed to teach the group

until the signal is given. All students should start and stop teaching together.

4. Conduct a whole-class review, outlining the important points that should have been made during each student's instruction, and allow students to be taught twice—once from a peer and then summarized by the teacher.

Make a checklist ahead of time of the critical concepts that each student should be teaching. As students teach, walk around the room and use a checklist to observe for those predetermined conceptual understandings.

Face-to-Face Interaction

According to Gregory and Parry (2006), students learn best when they are given the opportunity to participate in discussions in a nose-to-nose and toes-to-toes fashion. Decide whether you will organize your classroom desks into groups of four or five. It appears that as groups grow larger than five, students no longer feel pressured to contribute, which reduces positive interdependence and individual accountability (Dean et al., 2012). If seats are arranged in groups, cooperative work becomes easier since time does not have to be spent arranging desks. If not, teach students how to pick up their desks, move them into groups, and put them back when the cooperative activity is over. This is known as *forming* a group and must be practiced again and again until the arrangement becomes a habit. Students should sit in close enough proximity so that every member of the group can easily hear every other member of the group when discussion ensues. Students should also be able to maintain eye contact easily with one another. Students should practice talking only loud enough for their group members to hear their voices. They need to know that if you are capable of hearing one student's voice in the front of the room, that student is talking too loudly.

Interpersonal and Small-Group Social Skills

Most students do not come to class with built-in interpersonal or social skills that enable them to function easily in a group—that is, unless they have strong interpersonal intelligence. In fact, there appears to be an inverse relationship between society's dependence on social media and people's ability to communicate face to face. For cooperative groups to function effectively, specific social skills must be taught, just as specific content is taught. The social skills taught should be determined by the ones that student groups have difficulty demonstrating. The skills could include:

- Ensuring that every student in the group participates
- Paying close attention when a student is talking
- Critiquing a student's idea without putting down the student
- Encouraging other students to contribute

One of the best vehicles for teaching social skills is a T-chart. T-charts can be used to delineate what a social skill should look like and sound like when practiced. A sample visual of a T-chart is in figure 12.1.

Encouraging One Another

Looks Like	Sounds Like
Eye contact with speaker	"Good job!"
Smiles	"I hadn't thought of that."
Head nods	"Great idea!"
Leaning forward	"John, we haven't heard from you yet."

Figure 12.1: Sample T-chart.

Group Processing

If students are to improve their ability to work together, data should be collected to discover how well they practiced the social skills delineated in the previous section. Students should devote a portion of time at the end of the cooperative learning activity to examine the data and reach conclusions about what the data show. They can use observation checklists to gather the necessary data for discussion. There are at least two ways to gather the data. The process observer can fulfill this role by using the social skills checklist, figure 12.2 (page 136). Have this student list the names of students in the group down the left-hand side of the checklist and the social skill(s) to be observed across the top of the checklist. Every time a student in the group demonstrates one of the social skills, the process observer places a tally mark beside the student's name underneath the appropriate social skill. At the culmination of the cooperative task, allow about two minutes for the process observer to share the data with the group, and have the group reach conclusions about how well they practiced the given social skill.

Social Skills Checklist (Individual)			
Place a tally mark under the social skill(s) each student practices during the cooperative learning activity.			
Names	Paying Attention	Encouraging	Critiquing Ideas
1.			
2.			
3.			
4.			
5.			
6.			

Figure 12.2: Individual social skills checklist.

Visit www.learningsciences.com/bookresources for a reproducible version of this figure.

The teacher can also collect this data by using the social skills checklist (group), figure 12.3. The difference is that, rather than listing individual student names, the teacher lists group numbers down the left-hand side and the appropriate social skill across the top. Each time a student in the group exhibits one of the social skills, the teacher places a tally mark next to the group's number. Allow two minutes at the end of the cooperative learning task to give feedback to the class, indicating which groups were most successful at practicing the desired social skills. Do you know when you will have successfully improved the abilities of your students to work together? It will be the time when you see them using the social skills that you have taught them when there is no one observing to see whether they are doing so.

Social Skills Checklist (Group)			
Place a tally mark under the social skill(s) any member of a group practices during the cooperative learning activity.			
Groups	Contributing Ideas	Paraphrasing	Summarizing
1			
2			
3			
4			
5			
6			

Figure 12.3: Group social skills checklist.

Visit www.learningsciences.com/bookresources for a reproducible version of this figure.

Answer to Question 12

How do we know what students are learning when they work together?

Having students work effectively together capitalizes on their strengths or multiple intelligences. However, as society makes more use of social media as its prime method of communicating and face-to-face interactions take a back seat, it may become more difficult for students to work with one another to accomplish a task. It also becomes harder to derive a grade when students assist others during the formative process. Asking students to work cooperatively involves much more than just putting students in groups and expecting them to function. The five structures described in this chapter that foster cooperative interdependence are as follows: (1) positive interdependence, (2) individual accountability, (3) face-to-face interaction, (4) interpersonal and small-group social skills, and (5) group processing.

QUESTION 13

How Can Students Peer- and Self-Assess During the Formative Process?

Students need to know exactly how they are progressing toward any content-specific goal. That knowledge comes through specific feedback that the teacher usually provides. However, by the time a unit of study nears its end, students are in a better position to assess their personal learning or the learning of their classmates in relationship to a standard or objective.

Ainsworth and Viegut (2006) delineate the following benefits to the teacher, regarding students who are involved in their own assessment:

- Teacher time is saved since students are prescoring the assessments.

- Students are actively involved in examining their own work.

- Students learn to analyze their work as they consider whether it meets the expectations that they helped design.

- By looking at the work of their peers, students reinforce their own understanding of what they were expected to learn.

- Students can set goals for areas in need of future improvement.

- Students will feel a sense of ownership in the entire process.

Feedback is crucial to the brain, especially during the adolescent years. During that time, the brain undergoes the growth of new neurons, or memory cells, while the synapses, or connections between the neurons, are being pruned.

According to Sheryl Feinstein (2009), author of *Secrets of the Teenage Brain*, this feedback is just as crucial to memory as the original information sent to the brain, since students rarely understand things the first time they are taught. Repetition is crucial if information is to be remembered.

Without the information that feedback provides, students' brains won't know which neurons to grow and which to prune. As an added bonus, when the feedback is positive, neurotransmitters like serotonin and dopamine are released, which supply the student with feelings of calm and happiness and increase the likelihood that students will look forward to coming to class and raising their level of achievement.

Feinstein relates that in order to be meaningful, the feedback needs to be timely and specific. Assignments need to be graded and returned as soon as possible, with specific comments to accompany the grade given for the assignment. Remember when you were a college student and turned in a paper, you had to wait several weeks before receiving a grade. And remember when it was only a grade, with no comments? I don't know about you, but I always felt cheated if there were no comments. If the grade was an A, I always wanted to know what the professor liked about my effort so that I could repeat it in a subsequent assignment. If the grade was less than an A, I certainly needed comments so that I could ascertain what not to do next time. In fact, when researching the impact of grades on learning, Black and Wiliam (2009) found that students who received continuous feedback, without the grades, did up to 60 percent better than those students who received grades alone. It appeared that when students received both the grade and feedback on a paper or assignment, they were more interested in the grade and their ranking among their peers than on the feedback.

The more specific the comments, the better! I recall one occasion during my career as a curriculum specialist, when I was serving as the language arts coordinator for a large school system, and my supervisor fell behind on his annual evaluations of the staff. After conferencing with him, each of us soon discovered that every single coordinator had been given the same comments on his or her evaluation. We did not all do the same job nor with the same degree of proficiency. How important do you think those comments were to us? Many staff members discarded theirs after reading them.

Giving specific feedback is very time consuming for the teacher. One of a teacher's best assets will be the students themselves and their peers. Provide opportunities for students to reflect on their own performance and/or that of their classmates. However, students require a great deal of practice prior to being capable of assessing their learning or that of their peers. Greenstein (2010) recommends three guidelines for helping students to assess themselves and others.

Establish a Clear Purpose for the Peer or Self-Assessment

Is the purpose to enable students to reflect on their learning? Is the purpose to determine where student work stands in relation to a given standard? Is the purpose for students to identify areas of improvement and plan ways to actually improve? The strategy selected should align with the purpose of the assessment.

Share Clear Assessment Criteria With Students Early

If students are to evaluate how well their work meets established standards, they need to be perfectly clear on the criteria for measuring those standards. As discussed in chapter 11, students need to be shown what exemplary, high-quality work looks like. For example, it was found that rubrics created and scored by students enable them to focus their writing and think more critically about it (Algozzine et al., 2009).

They should also be shown work that does not exemplify quality, and they should engage in a discussion about why it does not meet expectations. Teachers can also document expectations by using rubrics that they develop or that students assist in developing.

Provide Students With Opportunities to Practice Constructive Feedback

Students need to know how to give their peers feedback that is constructive, specific, actionable, and supported by evidence from the product. These skills do not come easily to students; therefore, teachers should model giving this type of feedback and provide many opportunities for students to practice during the formative assessment phase. The following activities enable peers to provide feedback to one another.

Peer-Assessment Activities

Students should be taught how to assess their peers as well as themselves during the formative evaluation process. Students can be placed in groups for peer assessment. Helping students work with other students who may not necessarily be their best friends prepares them to exhibit the workplace competency of *interpersonal skills*, which they will need in order to work with people of diverse backgrounds. Whether to group in heterogeneous or homogeneous groups depends on the purpose of the task. In heterogeneous groups, students benefit from learning from one another. In homogeneous groups, extra support can be provided. These decisions should be based on the unique needs of each class. The following activities represent just a few of the ways that peers can determine whether other peers are learning.

Retelling

Have a student read aloud a piece of original writing to a peer. Ask the peer to retell in his or her own words what was just read and comment on a well-written part of the writing or one that was unclear. The comments should be very specific so that students tell exactly why the writing is good or why the writing is difficult to understand.

Homework Check

Place students in cooperative groups of four to six. Following an assignment that all groups complete, provide students with a rubric for assessing the assignment of another group. Students provide written feedback for one another.

Two Stars and a Wish

Whenever a student provides feedback to a peer on his or her work, the student has to provide two stars (positive statements about the work) and one wish (a recommendation for improving the work). Wiliam (2011) suggests that the comments be written on a Post-it note so, in case the student receiving the feedback does not find the feedback helpful, he or she can easily remove it from the work.

Homework Help Board

Have students post any questions they have about a homework assignment on a designated place in the room called the Homework Help Board. At the beginning of the day or period, students place on the board any questions they had about the homework. They sign their names on their papers. Students who feel that they can provide help with the homework should work with the students who have questions (Wiliam, 2011).

Rubrics

As evidenced in chapter 11, rubrics provide an excellent structure for defining criteria for a student's product or performance, or for evaluating content from the beginning of the unit to the end. Students can use rubrics to provide feedback to other students during the formative process. The terminology of the indicators should be kept simple and easy for all students to understand. A sample rubric for peer assessment in a high school technology classroom is provided in figure 13.1. This rubric was used by a computer graphics teacher at an International Baccalaureate (IB) School in Muscat, Oman, in the Middle East. Its purpose was to assess students' abilities to create and write about multiple computer graphic designs, while also demonstrating appropriate social skills. See chapter 11 for additional information on using rubrics as assessment tools.

Peer-Assessment Rubric	
6	• You drew more than six designs and did an excellent job of explaining whether each one matched your design specifications or not. • You used color with your designs. • You were always very interested and involved in what you were doing. • You worked extremely well on your own. • You showed that you knew a lot about working with others, safety, and respect.
5	• You drew at least six different designs and did quite a good job of explaining whether each one matched your design specifications or not. • You used color with most of your designs. • You were always interested in what you were doing. • You worked well on your own. • You showed that you knew quite a lot about working with others, safety, and respect.

continued ➡

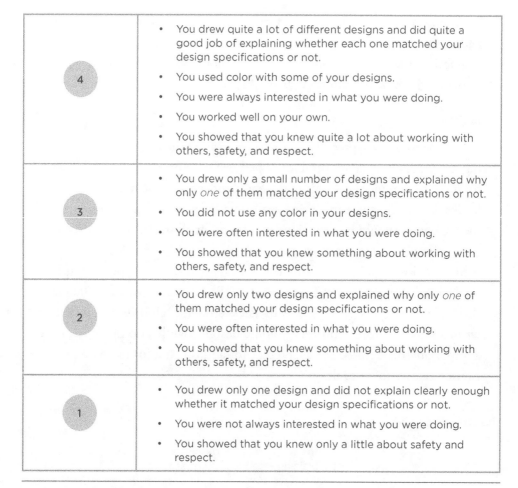

4	• You drew quite a lot of different designs and did quite a good job of explaining whether each one matched your design specifications or not. • You used color with some of your designs. • You were always interested in what you were doing. • You worked well on your own. • You showed that you knew quite a lot about working with others, safety, and respect.
3	• You drew only a small number of designs and explained why only *one* of them matched your design specifications or not. • You did not use any color in your designs. • You were often interested in what you were doing. • You showed that you knew something about working with others, safety, and respect.
2	• You drew only two designs and explained why only *one* of them matched your design specifications or not. • You were often interested in what you were doing. • You showed that you knew something about working with others, safety, and respect.
1	• You drew only one design and did not explain clearly enough whether it matched your design specifications or not. • You were not always interested in what you were doing. • You showed that you knew only a little about safety and respect.

Figure 13.1: A sample rubric for peer assessment in a high school technology classroom.

Critique the Idea, Not the Student

Students often have a difficult time critiquing another student's idea without criticizing the student himself or herself. A T-chart format, described in chapter 12 for teaching social skills, can be used for this purpose as well. A sample T-chart that is different from the previous one is in figure 13.2.

Self-Assessment Activities

John Hattie (2009) sums up the importance of self-assessment in the following statement: "The emphasis should be on what students can do, and then on students knowing what they are aiming to do, having multiple strategies for learning to do, and knowing when they have done it" (p. 199). The following

Critiquing Others' Ideas

Looks Like	Sounds Like
Eye contact with speaker	"I disagree."
Leaning forward	"Have you thought about . . .?"
One person speaking at a time	"Can you explain . . .?"
Asking questions for clarification	"Let me make sure I understand."
Looking confused	"How do you know that?"

Figure 13.2: Sample T-chart.

activities help all students reflect on their own progress toward predetermined standards or objectives.

Thinking Metacognitively

Students with intrapersonal intelligence will spend some class time thinking about their own thinking. According to Burke (2010), teachers can foster metacognition in all students by posing three questions that enable students to become self-reflective.

1. What do I already know about the concept or problem?

2. How can I break this concept or problem down into manageable parts or chunks?

3. Will I need the help of others to understand this concept or solve this problem?

Students can reflect on these questions and then verbalize the answers to a peer, the teacher, or in writing.

It's As Clear As Mud!

Have each student write on a Post-it note or an index card a point in the lesson that he or she simply did not understand. Collect the notes or cards and determine whether there are similarities in the points of misunderstanding. If so, reteach or clarify the confusions the following day for the entire class. Have students who do understand also hold two- or three-minute small-group reviews for students who need them.

Homework Self-Check

Provide students with a rubric that you developed or that students helped to develop, and have students grade their own in-class work or homework using the rubric.

Reflective Journals

Following a unit of study, have students write in a journal free-flowing reflections related to how well they feel they have mastered the unit's objectives or stated learning outcomes.

Journals With Prompts

Provide prompts for students to complete regarding what they learned and how they felt about the lesson. It may not be necessary for students to respond to each prompt. They may want to choose two or three, or the teacher can assign different prompts for different lessons. Some sample prompts follow.

- One thing I learned today is _____.

- One thing I liked most about this lesson was _____.

- I amazed myself when I _____.

- One thing I liked least about this lesson was _____.

- I am still unsure of _____.

- I want to find out more about _____.

- This lesson could have been improved if _____.

- One thing from this lesson that I can apply in my life is _____.

Answer to Question 13

How can students peer- and self-assess during the formative process?

A student who has strong intrapersonal intelligence is consistently self-assessing and reflecting on his or her skills and abilities. Near the end of a unit of study, all students would do well to engage in the same behavior. The timely and specific feedback that students—particularly adolescents—receive enables their brains to grow new memory cells and prune away unimportant connections. Students need to learn how to provide constructive feedback to their peers. Rubrics, T-charts, homework checks, and retellings are all activities for providing that crucial feedback. Reflective journals, metacognitive questions, and rubrics enable students to self-assess.

How Can Students Knock the Top Off Any Test?

We have come to the final chapter in this book. The brain theory of primacy/recency states that the brain remembers best the first thing it hears and remembers second best the last thing it hears. Therefore, you will remember the initial and final chapters of this book with more intensity than the medial chapters. This final chapter will provide a wonderful summary of the entire book since, regardless of everything we have discussed, there are basically four ways that teachers can give students a better chance of *knocking the top off* any teacher-made, end-of-course, standardized, or criterion-referenced test. Those four ways are as follows.

1. Teach all tested objectives.

2. Deliver instruction using twenty brain-compatible strategies.

3. Familiarize students with the test format.

4. Give students confidence to believe they will excel.

Teach All Tested Objectives

No, I am not asking you to teach the test! I am requesting that you ensure that students are taught the objectives on which they will be tested. Nothing destroys a student's confidence more than to sit down and take a test on material that has not been taught. Some students may have accidentally encountered the objective somewhere in their personal lives or educational career. These students have a decided advantage. Other students' experiences are limited, and they have had little to no familiarity with the standard or objective being taught. You will not know the difference in these two students without engaging them in one or more of the before-the-lesson activities delineated in chapter 7. To put all players on a level playing field, any objective to be assessed must be taught.

I am not for one minute suggesting that you teach *only* what is being tested. You should be teaching far more than that! However, what is being tested should have been taught. Let me make this clearer with a true story. I was working some years ago with an engaging teacher, the favorite teacher of most of her students. She taught in brain-compatible ways, and students learned so much during the school year. However, her students' test scores did not reflect the quality of her daily instruction. After examining her lesson plans and comparing them to objectives on which her students would be tested, we discovered something very important: what she was teaching and what was tested were two different things. As figure 14.1 shows, the objectives barely overlapped.

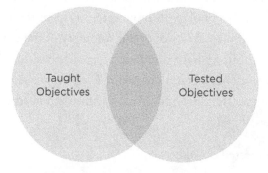

Figure 14.1: Tested objectives taught incorrectly.

What should have happened is depicted in figure 14.2. This teacher should have made sure that everything being tested was taught, and more. There is much more to know than that which is tested.

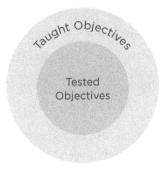

Figure 14.2: Tested objectives taught correctly.

We cannot expect students to show what they know if we have never taught them and taught them well! This brings us to the second way we can get students to score high on any test.

Deliver Instruction Using Twenty Brain-Compatible Strategies

After more than forty years in education, I am thoroughly convinced that neither textbooks nor computer programs matter; it is the *teacher* who makes the difference! Educational consultants and brain experts like Eric Jensen, David Sousa, and Judy Willis all relate that the way content is delivered has everything to do with how successful students will be during their formative and summative assessments.

More than twenty-five years ago, while working for a major school district, I discovered that, no matter the theory, there were basically twenty ways to deliver instruction. However, those twenty ways were not all contained in one book. So I wrote the book. That book became the best seller *Worksheets Don't Grow Dendrites: 20 Instructional Strategies That Engage the Brain.* The book is now in its third edition. Whether a teacher is teaching pre-K or calculus, or kindergarten or college, these strategies should be used to engage the brains of all students. They will help to ensure that students will score high on any test. The better news is that they also enable students to recall content long after the tests are over and make teaching and learning so much fun! Whether students are role-playing the steps in a math word problem, singing an original song to learn the original thirteen colonies, dancing out the stages of mitosis, or arranging themselves in sequential order to depict the sequence of events in a novel, students are learning, and that learning is evidenced when students are tested. Be certain that as instruction proceeds, those standards and objectives on which students are to be tested are taught in brain-compatible ways! Refer to chapter 4 for a list of the entire twenty engaging strategies.

Familiarize Students With the Test Format

If a concept is taught and reviewed in one way and tested in another, students may not make the brain connection between the way it was taught and the way it is being assessed. Therefore, it is important for students to be familiar with the vocabulary inherent in many standardized or criterion-referenced tests. According to Marzano and Kendall (1996), schools need to teach the vocabulary that students will see in the standards on state tests, since 85 percent of their success on these tests will be based on their knowledge of this vocabulary.

Oftentimes, students will know the answer to a question but may not comprehend the way in which that question is asked. Let's look at an example. When I teach the concept of main idea and details, I use the metaphor of a table and legs. The main idea is the top of the table and the legs are the supporting details. However, when taking standardized tests, students cannot draw a table and legs on the test booklet the way the student wanted to do in *First Grade Takes a Test*, the story mentioned in the introduction. Students can draw on their test booklet, but it will be thrown out. Then how is main idea tested? Oftentimes, test designers will ask any one of the following questions.

- What is the main idea of this story/poem?
- What is the best title for this story/poem?
- What is the theme of this story/poem?
- What is this story/poem mostly about?

Students need to know this terminology so that they will not be confused when the test is being administered. Chapman and King (2009) recommend that terms related to standardized testing be explained or defined in simple terms so that learners can experience comfort with them.

In another example, third-grade students in the school district I worked for scored exceptionally low on the math section of a standardized test. When analyzing test results, it was found that many students missed the questions dealing with approximation. You see, the question was asking students to select the answer that was the best approximation of the answer when two given numbers were added together. Students who were so used to choosing the correct answer were doing exactly that—selecting the correct answer (which was one of the answer choices) instead of the approximated answer. Once teachers knew this, they could spend more time helping students become familiar with the term *approximation* and practice problems where they were asked to select an approximate answer. During the next year, scores improved by fifty percentile points.

Give Students Confidence to Believe They Will Excel

In chapter 3, we discussed the negative impact of high stress or threat on the brain. Unfortunately, students and teachers have been under increased pressure to show evidence of high academic gains as measured by standardized and criterion-referenced test scores. Parents pressure students to make straight As and score high on the SAT or ACT. Students often put pressure on themselves to outdo their classmates academically. Yet, the brain research is clear. Cortisol, a hormone released when the brain is under severe threat, can keep the brain from forming a new memory or accessing memories that have already been formed (Allen & Currie, 2012).

If success breeds success, a student's confidence in his or her ability to do well on a test directly correlates to the level of success in his or her class performance when the information was being learned as well as the student's past test experiences. Students who lack self-confidence may manifest their weak belief system in a number of ways. They may experience test phobia. They may cheat to get the grades that they feel they otherwise would not receive. They may express their lack of caring about the test. Their sense of inadequacy is masqueraded by all of these feelings.

I recall a time when I was working on my doctorate and I took a statistics class. While I usually possess a modicum of confidence, I did not feel confident about taking a test in this subject. I sat in the back row of this class, although for other classes, I sat in the front. To be sure I was in the right place, I would glance at the computer screen of the person sitting beside me. By the way, I guess you could call that cheating! Word to the wise: when you cheat, be certain that the person you are cheating with is not confused as well. I even developed learned helplessness, where I would raise my hand and wait for my professor to assist me. When test time came, my grade was lower than usual, but so were the grades of the rest of the class, so we were allowed to retake the test. I experienced firsthand a true lack of confidence. It is a good thing that I was excelling in every other class I was taking at that time.

A brain-compatible classroom is one where students have experienced success from day one of class. It is one in which a variety of strategies enable students to master concepts and to show what they have learned through both traditional and authentic types of assessment. It is one where students have been told what they are expected to know, understand, and be able to do, and where both formative and summative types of assessments are used to determine if they know, understand, and can do it. When they take a test, students should be like athletes who are able to visualize success and are filled with the confidence to make that success happen!

Answer to Question 14

How can students knock the top off any test?

Four things must be in place for students to score high on any test. Those four things are as follows.

1. Be sure that all of the standards/objectives on which students are going to be tested have been taught.

2. Deliver instruction using twenty brain-compatible strategies that address all multiple intelligences and learning styles.

3. Familiarize students with the vocabulary, terminology, and test format that they will encounter on the test.

4. Give students the confidence to believe that they can excel!

Final Thoughts

Since storytelling is one of the most memorable brain-compatible strategies, allow me to conclude this book with two stories and an update.

Story I

Over fifteen years ago, I sat at the graduation ceremony of my nephew Isaac. His mother, Denise, sat next to me and cried from the beginning of the graduation exercises until the end. If I hadn't known better, I would have thought it was the graduate's funeral instead of his graduation from high school. While passing her one tissue after another, I decided to inquire about why she was so unhappy. She replied to me that the tears were not tears of unhappiness, but tears of joy! You see, it was not until a short time before graduation that Denise knew for sure that her son would graduate, and she was so relieved to see him walk across the stage and receive his diploma. Isaac, like my son, Chris, had struggled through high school.

Well, here is the rest of the story. Isaac graduated and immediately joined the air force. He has had a very successful career in the air force and has received multiple commendations for his ability to repair the guidance missile systems on jet fighter planes. In fact, I show a visual of one of his ceremonies in the class I teach. I don't believe you can be incompetent and yet receive commendations on your ability to do that job!

Like so many males, Isaac's gifts are his hands. He possesses Gardner's spatial intelligence. If more of his teachers had used strategies that enabled him to use that gift to learn content—strategies like drawing, manipulatives, technology, and project-based learning—as well as constructed-response test items, he might not have found high school so uninteresting and difficult. Isaac's initial test to join the military had been in a selected-response format. Every assessment since then has been performance based. Isaac excels on those more authentic types of assessment. If his portfolio had consisted of multiple types of assessments, his grades might not have been in question prior to graduation.

Story II

Jessica, my Anna Marie, did well on selected-response test items throughout her educational career. However, when she applied for the position of head chef of the banquet staff at the Ritz-Carlton Hotel, she had to demonstrate all three of the fundamental skills and three of the five workplace competencies on the SCANS report—a report where only 25 percent of the proficiencies are best assessed with traditional test items. Her initial assessment was a computerized selected-response test in which she was asked to demonstrate her ability to use basic skills in order to problem solve. A sample item from that test is as follows.

> Your spa sells facials at $20, massages at $50, and pedicures and manicures at $10. Fifteen percent of your clients buy facials, 5% massages, and 80% pedicures and manicures. You want to increase your profits by raising your prices. Which product should you increase?

Every other part of the assessment process consisted of constructed-response activities, including interviews with critical decision makers in the industry, in which she had to demonstrate her interpersonal skills. The preparation of a meal was evaluated according to a rubric measuring cleanliness and neatness during preparation, tastiness of food, and presentation of the meal.

The goal of schooling is to prepare students not only for success in school but, more important, in life. Unless we use brain-compatible strategies to teach students and include both traditional, selected-response items and authentic, constructed-response items during assessment, we will never prepare students for success in the world in which they must work and live.

Students need the capability of showing what they have learned in your class. Some will be able to accomplish that feat better on traditional selected-response test items. Others need the opportunity to create products and demonstrate knowledge through performances. Why not include both types if you really want to know whether students are learning? After all, isn't that what teaching and learning should be all about?

Update

Last, here is an update on the story with which I opened this book. Superior Court Judge Jerry Baxter, the judge in the cheating scandal, declared that he was uncomfortable with the seven-year prison terms he had previously handed down for three of the administrators who would not accept a plea deal and admit their guilt. Therefore, he reduced those three harshest sentences from seven years to three years of prison time with seven years of probation, $10,000 in fines, and two thousand hours of community service (Ellis & Lopez, 2015).

My hope is that this tragic occurrence will never be repeated! It was not only a travesty to the boys and girls who were deprived of valid summative assessments of their academic prowess but also to the educators who have now lost their livelihoods and freedom due to their blatant indiscretions. May this book help teachers and administrators realize that (1) if teachers, students, and parents know what students need to know, understand, and be able to do; (2) if brain-compatible engaging strategies are used to teach those things that they should know, understand, and be able to do; and (3) if multiple types of assessments are used to determine whether they can do it, this incident will never be repeated!

References

Ainsworth, L. (2015). *Common formative assessments 2.0: How teacher teams intentionally align standards, instruction, and assessment.* Thousand Oaks, CA: Corwin.

Ainsworth, L., & Viegut, D. (2006). *Common formative assessments: How to connect standards-based instruction and assessment.* Thousand Oaks, CA: Corwin.

Algozzine, B., Campbell, P., & Wang, A. (2009). *63 tactics for teaching diverse learners: Grades K–6.* Thousand Oaks, CA: Corwin.

Allen, R., & Currie, J. (2012). *U-turn teaching: Strategies to accelerate learning and transform middle school achievement.* Thousand Oaks, CA: Corwin.

Aungst, G. (2014). *Using Webb's depth of knowledge to increase rigor.* Retrieved from www.edutopia.org/blog/webbofknowledge.

Bacall, A. (2003). *The lighter side of technology in education.* Thousand Oaks, CA: Corwin.

Black, P., & Wiliam, D. (2009). Developing the theory of formative assessment. *Educational Assessment, Evaluation, and Accountability, 21*(1), 5–31.

Brookhart, S. M., & Nitko, A. J. (2007). *Assessment and grading in classrooms.* Upper Saddle River, NJ: Pearson.

Brualdi, A. C. (1998). *Classroom questions. ERIC/AE Digest* (ERIC Publications ERIC Digests in Full Text No. EDO-TM-98-02 RR93002002). Washington, DC: Eric Clearinghouse on Assessment and Evaluation.

Burke, K. (2010). *Balanced assessment: From formative to summative.* Bloomington, IN: Solution Tree.

Center for Excellence in Learning and Teaching. (n.d.) Revised Bloom's Taxonomy. Retrieved from http://www.celt.iastate.edu/teaching-resources/effective-practice/revised-blooms-taxonomy/

Chapman, C., & King, R. (2009). *Test success in the brain-compatible classroom* (2nd ed.). Thousand Oaks, CA: Corwin.

Cohen, M. (2006). *First grade takes a test.* New York: Star Bright Books.

Covey, S. (1996). *The 7 habits of highly effective people.* Salt Lake City, UT: Covey Leadership Center.

Dean, C. B., Hubbell, E. R., Pitler, H., & Stone, B. (2012). *Classroom instruction that works: Research-based strategies for increasing student achievement* (2nd ed.). Alexandria, VA: Association of Supervisors and Curriculum Directors.

Dillon, J. T. (1984). Research on questioning and discussion. *Educational Leadership, 42*(3), 50–56.

Ellis, R., & Lopez, E. (2015). *Judge reduces sentences for 3 educators in Atlanta cheating scandal.* Retrieved from http://www.cnn.com/2015/04/30/us/atlanta-schools-cheating-scandal/

Feinstein, S. G. (2009). *Secrets of the teenage brain: Research-based strategies for reaching and teaching today's adolescents.* Thousand Oaks, CA: Corwin.

Fogarty, R. (2009). *Brain-compatible classrooms* (3rd ed.). Thousand Oaks, CA: Corwin.

Gardner, H. (1983). *Frames of mind: The theory of multiple intelligences.* New York: Basic Books.

Green, L. S., & Casale-Giannola, D. (2011). *40 active learning strategies for the inclusive classroom, grades K–5.* Thousand Oaks, CA: Corwin.

Greenstein, L. (2010). *What teachers really need to know about formative assessment.* Alexandria, VA: Association of Supervisors and Curriculum Directors.

Gregory, G. H., & Chapman, C. (2013). *Differentiated instructional strategies: One size doesn't fit all.* (3rd ed.). Thousand Oaks, CA: Corwin.

Gregory, G. H., & Parry, T. (2006). *Designing brain-compatible learning* (3rd ed.). Thousand Oaks, CA: Corwin.

Haladyna, T. M. (1997). *Writing test items to evaluate higher-order thinking.* Boston: Allyn & Bacon.

Harris, M. J., & Rosenthal, R. (1985). Mediation of interpersonal expectancy effects: 31 meta-analyses. *Psychological Bulletin, 97*(3), 363–386.

Hattie, J. (2012). *Visible learning for teachers: Maximizing impact on learning.* London: Routledge.

Hattie, J. A. C. (2009). *Visible learning: A synthesis of over 800 meta-analyses relating to achievement.* London: Routledge.

Hattie, J. A. C., & Jaeger, R. (1998). Assessment and classroom learning: A deductive approach. *Assessment in Education Principles, Policy, and Practice, 5*(1), 111–122.

Hiebert, J., Gallimore, R., Garnier, H., Givvin, K. B., Hollingsworth, H., Jacobs, J. K., et al. (2003). *Teaching mathematics in seven countries: Results from the TIMSS 1999 video study* (NCES No. 2003-013). Washington, DC: National Center for Education Statistics.

James, A. N. (2015). *Teaching the male brain: How boys think, feel, and learn in school* (2nd ed.). Thousand Oaks, CA: Corwin.

Jensen, E. (2000). Moving with the brain in mind. *Educational Leadership, 58*(3), 34–37.

Jensen, E. (2001). *Arts with the brain in mind.* Thousand Oaks, CA: Corwin.

Jensen, E. (2008). *Brain-based learning: The new paradigm of teaching.* Thousand Oaks, CA: Corwin.

Jensen, E., & Dabney, E. (2000). *Learning smarter: The new science of teaching.* San Diego, CA: The Brain Store.

Johnson, D. W., & Johnson, R. T. (2002). Learning together and alone: Overview and meta-analysis. *Asia Pacific Journal of Education, 22*(1), 95–105.

Lowry, D. (2015). Sentences reduced for 3 in cheating scandal. Retrieved April 30, 2015, from http://www.usatoday.com/story/news/nation/2015/04/30/atlanta-educators-resentenced/26643997/

Marzano, R. J. (2010). *Formative assessment and standards-based grading.* Bloomington, IN: Marzano Research Laboratory.

Marzano R. J., & Kendall, J. S. (1996). *Designing standards-based districts, schools, and classrooms.* Alexandria, VA: Association for Supervision and Curriculum Development.

McLaughlin, M., & Overturf, B. J. (2013). *The Common Core: Teaching K–5 students to meet the reading standards.* Newark: DE: International Reading Association.

Medina, J. (2008). *Brain rules: 12 principles for surviving and thriving at work, home, and school.* Seattle, WA: Pear Press.

Multiple Intelligences of Adult Literacy and Education. (n.d.). Assessment: Find your strengths. *Literacy Works.* Retrieved from www.literacyworks.org/mi/assessment/

Pay closer attention: Boys are struggling academically. (December 2, 2004). *USA Today*, p. 12A.

Rosenthal, R., & Jacobson, L. (1968). *Pygmalion in the classroom: Teacher expectation and pupils' intellectual development.* New York: Holt, Rinehart, and Winston.

Rosenthal, R., & Rubin, D. B. (1978). Interpersonal expectancy effects: The first 345 studies. *Behavioral and Brain Sciences, 1*(3), 377–415.

Rowe, M. B. (1986, January–February). Wait time: Slowing down may be a way of speeding up! *Journal of Teacher Education, 37*(1), 43–50.

Secretary's Commission on Achieving Necessary Skills. (1991). What work requires of schools. *A SCANS report for America 2000.* Washington, DC: US Department of Labor.

Sousa, D. A. (2006). *How the brain learns* (3rd ed.). Thousand Oaks, CA: Corwin.

Sousa, D. A. (2011). *How the brain learns* (4th ed.). Thousand Oaks, CA: Corwin.

Sprenger, M. (2007). *Becoming a "wiz" at brain-based teaching: How to make every year your best year* (2nd ed.). Thousand Oaks, CA: Corwin.

Stiggins, R. (2014). *Revolutionize assessment: Empower students, inspire learning.* Thousand Oaks, CA: Corwin.

Tanner, M. L., & Cassados, I. (1998). Writing to learn. In J. Irwin & M. Doyle (Eds.). *Reading/writing connections: Learning from research* (pp. 145–159). Newark, DE: International Reading Association.

Tate, M. L. (2010). *Worksheets don't grow dendrites: 20 instructional strategies that engage the brain* (2nd ed.). Thousand Oaks, CA: Corwin.

Tate, M. L. (2014). *Reading and language arts worksheets don't grow dendrites: 20 literacy strategies that engage the brain* (3rd ed.). Thousand Oaks, CA: Corwin.

Tate, M. L. (2016). *Worksheets don't grow dendrites: 20 instructional strategies that engage the brain* (3rd ed.). Thousand Oaks, CA: Corwin.

Thomas, R. (2014). *A simple and effective student engagement strategy: Praise, prompt, and leave.* Retrieved from http://edge.ascd.org/blogpost/a-simple-and-effective-student-engagement -strategy-praise-prompt-and-leave

Thompson, H. (n.d.). *Taxonomy.* Retrieved from https://educatingmatters.wordpress.com /taxonomy/

Tileston, D. W. (2011). *Closing the RTI gap: Why poverty and culture count.* Bloomington, IN: Solution Tree Press.

Van Lier, I. (1998). The relationship between consciousness, interaction, and language learning. *Language Awareness, 7*(2/3), 128–143.

Wagner, T. (2008, October). Rigor redefined. *Educational Leadership, 66*(2), 20–24.

Walsh, J. A., & Sattes, B. D. (2005). *Quality questioning: Research-based practice to engage every learner*. Thousand Oaks, CA: Corwin.

Wiggins, G. P., & McTighe, J. (2005). *Understanding by design* (Expanded 2nd ed.). Alexandria, VA: Association for Supervision and Curriculum Development.

Wilen, W. W. (1991). *Questioning skills for teachers: What research says to the teacher* (2nd ed.). Washington, DC: National Education Association.

Wiliam, D. (2007). Content then process: Teacher learner communities in the service of formative assessment. In D. Reeves (Ed.), *Ahead of the curve: The power of assessment to transform teaching and learning*. Bloomington, IN: Solution Tree Press.

Wiliam, D. (2011). *Embedded formative assessment*. Bloomington, IN: Solution Tree Press.

Willis, J. (2006). *Research-based strategies to ignite student learning*. Alexandria, VA: Association for Supervision and Curriculum Development.

Index

W

wall charts
    Carousel, 103
    Draw It!, 103
    Solve It!, 97
Walsh, Jackie A., 64, 69
Webb, Norman, 68
Wiliam, Dylan, 11, 12, 45, 119, 142
Willis, Judy, 33, 118, 151
Woods, Tiger, 34
Word Smart. *see* intelligence, linguistic

CPSIA information can be obtained
at www.ICGtesting.com
Printed in the USA
LVHW06s1542280618
582180LV00011B/97/P

9 781941 112311